VOCATIONAL EDUCATION AND TRAINING

Patrick Ainley

CASSELL

Cassell Educational Limited
Villiers House
41/47 Strand
London WC2N 5JE
England

© Cassell Educational Limited 1990

First published 1990

British Library Cataloguing in Publication Data
Ainley, Patrick
  Vocational education and training – (Education matters)
  1. Great Britain. Vocational education
  I. Title II. Series
  370.1130941

ISBN 0-304-31942-2 (hardback)
     0-304-31948-1 (paperback)

Typeset by Input Typesetting Ltd, London

Printed and bound in Great Britain by
Biddles Ltd, Guildford and King's Lynn

Col. B 0765 /5.95. 7.90

VOCATIONAL EDUCATION

AND TRAINING

BOOKS IN THIS SERIES

CONTENTS

'We go upon the practical mode of teaching, Nickleby; the regular education system. C-l-e-a-n, clean, verb active, to make bright, to scour. W-i-n, win, d-e-r, der, winder, a casement. When the boy knows this out of the book, he goes and does it. It's just the same principle as the use of the globes. Where's the second boy?'

'Please sir, he's weeding the garden', replied a small voice.

'To be sure', said Squeers, by no means disconcerted. 'So he is. B-o-t, bot, t-i-n, tin, bottin, n-e-y, ney, bottiney, noun substantive, a knowledge of plants. When he has learned that bottiney means a knowledge of plants, he goes and knows 'em. That's our system, Nickleby; what do you think of it?'

'It's a very useful one, at any rate', answered Nicholas significantly.

FOREWORD

Professor E. C. Wragg, Exeter University

During the 1980s a succession of Education Acts changed considerably the nature of schools and their relationships with the outside world. Parents were given more rights and responsibilities, including the opportunity to serve on the governing body of their child's school. The 1988 Education Act in particular, by introducing for the first time a National Curriculum, the testing of children at the ages of 7, 11, 14 and 16, local management, including financial responsibility and the creation of new types of school, was a radical break with the past. Furthermore the disappearance of millions of jobs, along with other changes in our society, led to reforms not only of schools, but also of further and higher education.

In the wake of such rapid and substantial changes it was not just parents and lay people, but also teachers and other professionals working in education, who found themselves struggling to keep up with what these many changes meant and how to get the best out of them. The *Education Matters* series addresses directly the major topics of reform, such as the new curriculum, testing and assessment, the role of parents and the handling of school finances, considering their effects on primary, secondary, further and higher education, and also the continuing education of adults.

The aim of the series is to present information about the challenges facing education in the remainder of the twentieth century in an authoritative but readable form. The books in the series, therefore, are of particular interest to parents, governors and all those concerned with education, but are written in such a way as to give an overview to students, experienced teachers and other professionals who work in the field.

Each book gives an account of the relevant legislation and background, but, more importantly, stresses practical implications of change with specific examples of what is being or can be done to make reforms work effectively. The authors are not only authorities in their field, but also have direct experience of the matters they write about. That is why the *Education Matters* series makes an important contribution to both debate and practice.

ACKNOWLEDGEMENTS

With thanks to Professor John Bynner of City University Social Statistics Research Unit and Professor Tony Edwards of Newcastle University Department of Education for their trouble in reading through and commenting upon the draft. Also to Elliot Stern who monitors the Enterprise in Higher Education Initiative at the Tavistock Institute; Charles Harvey, formerly at the Central London Careers Office, for his help with Careers Service matters; Alan Brown of Surrey University's Department of Educational Studies for his valuable criticisms of my rosy view of NCVQ; and to Lucy Ball, the Director of Youthaid, for bringing me up to date with the latest developments in Youth Training. Also to John Abbott, the Director of Education 2000 and the pupils and teachers of all the secondary schools in Letchworth, at Mons School, Dudley, and St Paul's Way, London.

INTRODUCTION

Education is never for its own sake, whatever people often pretend. Schooling, in particular, prepares future generations for the type of society which their elders think they will and should inherit. The curriculum contains a selection from present knowledge that is intended to be useful in the future. The habits and morality that schools also attempt to instil are those which the older generation thinks are appropriate for the young.

For individuals, their studies, even if pursued to the highest level solely out of personal interest, affect the range of occupational choice available to them. Even the most obscure scientific research, followed merely for the sake of knowledge itself, may turn out to have applications in technical invention. Artistic creation finds its imitation in design, while philosophical reflection can also have profound practical consequences.

These connections are often hidden. Vocational education makes them explicit. Since 1976 government policy has aimed to bring the education system as a whole more directly in line with the changing labour needs of industry and commerce. In particular, the ascendancy of the Department of Employment's Manpower Services Commission brought sweeping changes to education at all levels. Now that the Department of Education has regained control through the centralising measures of the 1988 Education Reform Act, this book briefly surveys what is left of the vocational phase of education policy in our schools and colleges. It concentrates upon the secondary schools and the new training arrangements that have been made for students in their last years of compulsory education; these are examined in relation to the changes which have occurred in the labour market and which are continuing to transform not only work, but society in general.

If assessment of some vocational and other educational programmes may sometimes seem negative, it aims to be realistic. Intentions are measured against outcomes, and description deliberately avoids the sort of elastic language in which these programmes are often represented so as to span what are inevitably areas of political contention and debate. Instead, the implications of a changing labour market are teased out, together with the demands that this new division of labour makes upon the youngest entrants to the workforce and for those who prepare them in the schools and colleges for the work that will sustain society in the future.

First, the key terms of the new vocational education are presented and discussed and the history of their recent introduction reviewed before examining different examples of vocational education and training. Throughout the book these are illustrated by descriptions of different schools, colleges and training institutions where they have been implemented.

The survey of current vocational education and training begins with a consideration of how the innovations of the vocational period from 1976 to 1987 have been incorporated into the National Curriculum. The Technical and Vocational Education Initiative (TVEI) is now supposed to support this curriculum. Its development is traced from its launch in 1983.

The City Technology Colleges are in some ways the successors to TVEI and represent the more differentiated system of vocational schooling which it is the aim of the 1988 Act to encourage. They are examined, along with the Youth Training Scheme (renamed Youth Training in April 1990) and what has become of it in the new conditions of employment and demography at the beginning of the 1990s.

The closer relations of education with industry and commerce are preserved in some of the institutional arrangements of the 1988 Act, which require representation by local business on the governing boards of all schools and colleges. Previously these links had been developed through work experience for many school pupils along with programmes of careers education. These have been formalised by 'Compacts' between schools and local employers. New vocational qualifications have been introduced and there is a continuing effort to standardise these which has radical implications for education in the future and for the selection, reward and training of all employees.

As well as the qualifications necessary to find employment in particular occupations, there has also been a growth of pre-vocational education and training to communicate the skills and knowledge required for entry to all jobs and for further progression in them. These pre-vocational skills are described along with the programmes that aim to teach them. A different level of pre-vocational knowledge is demanded of those remaining or returning to further and higher education to prepare for entry to a narrower range of more specialised occupations and also for professional employment. Vocational education and training in these sectors of education is also briefly reviewed.

Finally, the vocational and training schemes of two European countries which are in many ways very similar to England and Wales are compared to bring out the contrasting arrangements that they make to align their education systems with their economies – in Germany's case, an economy that is much stronger, and in Scotland's somewhat weaker, than the UK norm.

In summary, the possibility is presented of a new, coherent vocational education and training for all which is geared to rapid technological change, economic modernisation and democratic control. This is intended as a contribution to what is and will surely continue to be a debate, not only about education and training, but about the whole future development of society.

To reduce clutter, footnotes and references are omitted. However, a short bibliography is appended to enable readers to follow up any items of particular interest to them.

Chapter 1
OVERVIEW: EDUCATION AND EMPLOYMENT

Key words

Society is changing with unprecedented rapidity. New technology is not only transforming work itself but offering new ways of learning. It has changed what we do and how we think about it. These changes are reflected in our use of words. Nowadays, for instance, nobody has a job anymore; everyone has a career.

Job used to be how most people referred to the way they earned their wages. Now it is coming to mean only a particular item of work, like a batch of calculations submitted to a computer. *Career*, once meaning literally a crazy, erratic course (like a horse charging about), has broadened out from referring only to the meteoric rise and fall of stage entertainers and politicians. Now it embraces any occupation with predictable and regular increases in salary and responsibilities. These secure posts were previously the preserve of the self-regulating professions. Today these prospects are supposed to apply to all occupations. Monthly salary cheques replacing weekly cash wages for the majority of employees signal this transformation.

Rapid technological change also means that few people can expect to do the same work throughout their lives. As the government pointed out in a 1988 White Paper on *Employment for the 1990s*, 'Seven out of 10 of the work force who will be at work in the year 2000 are already at work, but the great majority of them will not be doing the same job in the year 2000 as they are doing today'. An individual career thus comes to mean how you move through life from one job to another and can also include periods of unemployment and retraining.

Work is more than a job but, whether job or career, wage or salary, work is still, as they say, a four-letter word. Despite all the perennial speculations about the loss of the work ethic, its meaning is unlikely to change as long as the vast majority of us have to work in order to gain the means to live and some access to society's resources. This is what gives such salience to any discussion of education and employment.

As has often been pointed out, the use of the word work has become restricted in our society to paid labour only. Recently however, the contributions made by unpaid labour, for example in housework, or by caring in the community, have been recognised to some extent. The new world of work, with new technologies bringing new patterns of working and new demands for learning at work, challenges the traditional boundaries that have been drawn around education. If education is really to be a lifelong process, it can no longer stop at a certain age – 16 or 18 for the majority, 21 for a minority.

Training is the keyword that has been virtually remodelled to fit the new circumstances. Like *schooling*, it once referred to the drills and routines instilled by the rewards and punishments of rote learning. Horses were schooled and circus animals trained. But now training has taken over some of the broader meanings of education. Originally, *education* meant a leading out or initiation into the adult world. Yet education is no longer enough, as people are expected to train and retrain throughout their lives in order to keep pace with the new technology that is continually being introduced.

Vocation, like education, has a noble and lofty ancestry. It was literally a call from God to follow a particular path in life, especially into the priesthood. Today the new trinity of Vocational Education and Training is supposed to prepare the entire workforce for a flexible future of rapid and unpredictable change. Like so many of the new creations of the latest technical revolution, it has its own acronym, VET.

Pre-vocational is another of these new key terms attached to education and training. It is often used interchangeably with vocational. Some effort will be made in this book to

5

distinguish between the two words and to examine their different meanings at various levels of education.

Vocational education does not pretend to pursue purely disinterested knowledge. It sets out to construct a school and college system that prepares its entrants for future employment. A course of study that leads to employment in one specific occupation is strictly vocational. At the other end of the scale, curricula that aim to communicate the common theoretical knowledge and practical skills required of all entrants to employment are in effect pre-vocational.

All education is a mixture of these two elements. It tends to be pre-vocational in the initial stages and to selectively become more narrowly vocational in the later stages. With the accelerating introduction of new technology, the specific vocational skills required for many specialised jobs and the pre-vocational abilities and knowledge needed for nearly all work, as well as to participate effectively in society, are changing rapidly.

To show how quickly words change to reflect new realities, it is remarkable to recall that during the 1960s the Association of Heads of Secondary Technical Schools decided they should change the name of their schools. The terms technical and vocational, they thought, ought no longer to be used because 'these words were debased . . . by their practical and working-class connotations'. Only twenty years later, the government launched an initiative aimed at bringing vocational and technical education to every secondary school and further education college in the country. Technology now forms a part of the National Curriculum, and Youth Training aims to give vocational technical training to all young workers.

VET promises access to new careers using new technology, processing information instead of directly handling the tools that turn raw materials into manufactured objects. As the hard manual labour and craft skills of the past are increasingly undertaken by machines, programmed and monitored by non-manual operators, the distinctions between manual and mental labour are also breaking down. This is undermining the fundamental distinction between those who work with their hands and those who work with their brains, upon which rests the entire crumbling edifice of the antique British class system.

Traditional definitions of class are weakening; more people describe themselves as 'middle class' and fewer as 'working class'. The expansion of offices and businesses has put more people into this 'non-manual' category, while in the growing service sector of the economy, interpersonal skills are increasingly required. The skills of handling people instead of products are needed, not only to provide personal services but also to sell them to the customer in the first place.

Thus *personal and social skills* are among the skills that VET offers to those who undertake it, which nowadays includes nearly everybody. For during the 1980s VET penetrated down from the secondary schools into the primaries. It also expanded upwards for the growing numbers staying on beyond school-leaving age to enter youth training or to go on to further or higher education.

Indeed, to acquire the new skills needed for the new work with new technology, training and retraining throughout working life is now held to be essential for everybody. It is important not just for individuals but for the future and international competitiveness of the country; for, despite all the effort that has been put into training and retraining in recent years, 'skill shortages' are everywhere reported as still putting the brakes on economic advance and industrial modernisation.

To use new technology effectively in competition with international rivals, employers and government continually emphasise the need for flexibility in the workforce. People must become *multi-skilled* in order to apply the skills they acquire through VET in the many different areas where new technology is used. They can no longer restrict themselves to one particular area of expertise where new technology will take over their craft and perform it more efficiently and quickly.

Traditional skilled craftsmen – carpenters are the classic

example – typically own their own tools and hire themselves out for a specific job. Unlike them, multi-skilled workers carry their transferable skills in their hands and heads. They use them wherever they are required on work that the application of new technology renders more similar and more simple. Potentially they can therefore apply themselves to a wider range of tasks, avoiding dull routine and repetitive hard labour.

Multi-skilled working as it actually occurs in industry today does not always equal the intensity of effort and application embodied in the old craft skills. In many cases it represents de-skilling towards semi-skilled, undifferentiated working. Professor Charles Handy in his book *The Future of Work* quotes the personnel manager of a large American automobile plant who used to boast that they could take anyone off the street and train him to do a job on the assembly line in one-and-a-half hours. Even with new 'post-Fordist' methods of working, a recent article in *American Machinist* recommends employing retarded people with a mental age of 12 to operate the latest numerically controlled machine tools.

The range of different tasks and occupations in society is constantly increasing. This happens both as new scientific discoveries and technical innovations are applied and as old handicrafts, if they are not completely lost, are preserved for a luxury art and craft market. But whether this means that the average person has become more skilful, both at work and when using the more and more sophisticated labour-saving and pleasure-inducing devices of the electronic home, is another question.

Critics label ours a society of passive consumers, where even the social skills of good neighbourliness and co-operation at work are being lost to individual isolation and competition. Enthusiasts point to the variety of lifestyles and leisure pursuits that more people now enjoy. These exercise new skills outside the confines of work and in the context of sports and recreation. So it is not clear whether society as a whole is in fact becoming more or less skilled. Certainly many skills have been irretrievably lost. The great traditions of the past which have died out can never be re-created to equal the master craftsmen who raised the cathedrals of Europe, or those who created the finest art of other lost cultures and civilisations throughout the world. But it may be that new technology offers us a unique opportunity to build upon their achievements because it can remove the repetitious drudgery of past production yet allow many more people to recreate the fine detail and bold imagination of traditional crafts with new materials.

We can begin to grasp these possibilities by looking briefly at the recent history of education and training.

Key dates

Efforts have been made to create a coherent system of education and training in England and Wales since Elizabethan times. Yet, strangely for the countries that launched the industrial revolution upon the world, the 1563 Statute of Artificers was the only legislation to deal exclusively with training for work until the Industrial Training Act became law in 1964.

During its industrial heyday British education was dominated by the classics, while technology and commerce were regarded as merely vulgar. The men who ruled the Empire were brought up on a diet of Latin and Greek in their public and grammar schools. The Board schools aimed only to instil morality and literacy into the labouring masses. The result was that schools and colleges put a premium on intellectual and abstract knowledge as opposed to practical skills. Formal training was seen as a second-class method of instruction while apprenticeships, which had grown from their medieval origins under the control of the workers themselves, remained the route to the coveted status of skilled craftsman for manual employees. These attitudes still persist today.

There was a break in this dismal record between 1939 and 1945, when more than half a million people, many of them women, were drafted into government training courses to streamline industry for all-out war production. After the war, technical schools were included as part of the tripartite system of education established by the 1944 Education Act. Pupils were allocated to either grammar, technical or secondary modern schools on the basis of an 'intelligence' test in the form of the 11-plus exam.

These three types of school were intended to correspond to the divisions of labour between non-manual, skilled or unskilled manual work. These traditional divisions of labour in manufacturing industry were already breaking down after the war and they became virtually obsolete with the introduction of new technology. In any case, the technical schools were under-funded and remained very much second-best, along with the secondary moderns, where some practical subjects were also taught – mainly woodwork and metalwork for the boys and 'housecraft' (sometimes elevated to 'domestic science') for the girls. Then, during the 1960s and 1970s, the 'techs' were absorbed into the new comprehensive schools. These set out to beat the grammar schools at their own game of formal, academic education. The grammar schools in turn tried to prove the equal of the most prestigious public schools in the unequal competition to get as many pupils as possible into university.

The expansion of the universities in the 1960s catered mainly for middle-class youth, offering them a route to preferred non-manual employment in the growing service and state sectors. Despite their elders' agonising over the dangers of a gap between the 'two cultures' of art and science, these students persisted in their preference for the arts over the sciences and their practical applications. The polytechnics, modelled on a Soviet ideal of combining practical and theoretical study, quickly came to be imitations of the other new universities.

What remained of technical education in formal institutions took place largely in night schools and further education colleges. Here it became a predominantly part-time education for students working in factories and offices. Meanwhile the informal and very varied procedures of time-served apprenticeships remained the main route to acquiring craft skills for skilled manual work. Numbers of apprentices peaked in 1966, although the proportion of young workers apprenticed did not decline until its highest, 25 per cent, in 1969 – a third of all boys but less than a tenth of girls, and those were mainly hairdressers.

Especially for young, working-class men, apprenticeships still sorted the skilled, regularly employed breadwinner from the insecure and unskilled labourer. Just as in Victorian times, apprenticeships under the control of the trade unions guarded an aristocracy of labour, as distinguished from the rough mass of the unskilled. Distinct labour markets thus remained based upon divisions of class, sex, age and race.

As trade unions represented not only skilled trades but also large general unions, the labour movement collectively argued for a comprehensive education and training system. However, this demand was undermined by the actual way in which new technology was introduced into industry. Britain's employers did not win the agreement and co-operation of their workers for change but instead faced defensive union determination to stick to long-established working practices. Where employers could overcome this opposition, new methods of production resulted in overall shedding and de-skilling of labour. The industrial heartlands of Britain plainly showed the consequences of such an application of new technology. There was mass redundancy of the old craft skills and their replacement, if they were replaced, by semi-skilled working in new 'service' industries. Whole communities were destroyed, along with the patterns of life reproduced over decades in relation to traditional ways of working.

These changes had been undermining the foundations of society for a long time. During the 1960s, change was greeted enthusiastically by the Labour Prime Minister, Harold Wilson, whose policies promoted the new society that was being forged in 'the white heat of technological revolution'. His government began to introduce comprehensive schools on a wide scale. These schools were intended to give equal opportunities for all their pupils to take fullest advantage of the new economic modernisation that was planned.

As for training, a Conservative government set up the Manpower Services Commission in 1974 to co-ordinate the Industrial Training Boards which, since the Industrial Training Act, had overseen training arrangements in each particular industry. But as unemployment rose during the 1970s, a Labour government used the MSC to run temporary employment schemes, especially for the increasing numbers of young people leaving school without immediate prospects of getting work. This rise in youth unemployment threatened a crisis of confidence in the secondary schools, where teachers could no longer hold out the carrot of a good job through hard work for examinations.

The last Labour Prime Minister, James Callaghan, therefore redefined the purpose of education in a 1976 speech given at the trade-union sponsored Ruskin College in Oxford. Callaghan said that schools and colleges were out of touch with the changing world of work and blamed them for not teaching the attitudes and abilities which would help their students to get jobs when they left. This speech changed the agenda of education for a decade. Instead of aiming at the all-round development of pupils through open entry to comprehensive schools, education concentrated upon vocational preparation for work that was actually available to fewer and fewer school leavers. In place of equal opportunities, 'relevance' to the world of work became the new watchword for schools.

After the 1981 urban riots convinced Margaret Thatcher that youth unemployment could no longer be ignored, her government took up and vastly expanded the new plan for education that had been outlined by Mr Callaghan. Make-work schemes such as the Youth Opportunities Programme had been introduced by Labour as part of its social contract with the trade union leaders in exchange for their damping down the wage demands of their members. Such schemes for the young unemployed were now used by the Conservatives as an opportunity to introduce a national system of youth training for all school-leavers, whether employed or unemployed, and of retraining for all adults. These goals were set by the government for the MSC's New Training Initiative in 1981.

The Youth Training Scheme began as a one-year foundation course in 1983 and added a second year in 1985. It was intended to be a modernised apprenticeship for all school-leavers. For those still at school, the government introduced the Technical and Vocational Education Initiative for 14–18-year-olds in 1983 and new courses and examinations were produced for new non-academic sixth-formers. City Technology Colleges, first suggested in 1986, were supposed to specialise in the new skills required for high technology, reintroducing the old tripartite divisions in a fresh form. Work experience (for both teachers and pupils) was expanded along with schools' links with industry. As well as vocational skills, pupils, even at primary level, were encouraged to develop the attitudes needed to run their own businesses by attending 'economic awareness' courses and by setting up mini-enterprises in school. Traditional apprenticeship and day-release courses in further education colleges were boosted by non-advanced further education for swelling numbers of students. In higher education the MSC launched a £100 million programme intended to bring the benefits of enterprise to all students in every subject.

Finally, the 1988 Education Reform Act introduced a National Curriculum which guaranteed science and technology to all pupils. However, this curriculum, hastily drafted before the 1987 election, also rehashed the traditional subject divisions that had formed the basis of pre-war grammar schooling (pre-First World War! – it largely followed the 1904 recommendations for grammar schools). The tests that were devised for it and the system of competition which it aimed to foster between schools could only encourage rote learning of abstract facts and figures over their practical applications. For the whole emphasis was now upon the basic standards of education that were supposed to have been lost in the previous comprehensive reform and in the enthusiasm for practical skills.

The fall in the numbers of school-leavers and the simultaneous partial recovery of the economy from recession created a sudden shortage of labour in the prosperous parts of the country. YTS as a unified, national apprenticeship scheme fell apart, as the government abandoned the consensus upon which it had been built by making entry compulsory with the withdrawal of the right to benefits for those under age 18 without work. This ensured that the scheme in general would remain a last resort for the young unemployed, a two-year successor to YOP, as its critics had originally predicted.

The government also used the refusal of the 1988 Trades Union Congress to participate in the Employment Training scheme for adults to wind up the Manpower Services Commission. It was reabsorbed into its parent Department of Employment, while vocational training reverted to the employers who in the past had never regarded it as their first priority. Plans for a super-Ministry of Education and Training were shelved and the Department of Education and Science regained undisputed central control over schools and colleges. The vocational phase in education introduced by the 1976 Ruskin speech was over. What is left of it in schools and colleges will now be briefly examined.

Chapter 2

ASPECTS OF VOCATIONALISM

Vocational and technical education in the National Curriculum

The 'Great Reform' of education promised by the Conservatives in the 1987 general election and subsequently embodied in the 1988 Education Reform Act was intended to raise basic standards in state schools. It was sold to the educational establishment of teachers and administrators who have to make it work as offering for the first time an entitlement for all pupils to study every subject in a new National Curriculum. These subjects include not only the 'core' of English, maths and science but also the 'foundation' of history, geography, art, music, technology, physical education and a foreign (major European) language.

To this 'basic curriculum' was added – during the Bill's passage through the House of Lords – religious instruction and a collective act of 'predominantly Christian' worship. Although these clauses of the Act are hardly directly relevant to a multicultural and predominantly secular society, the rest of the National Curriculum was presented as essential education for the new society of high technology and flexible employment. Girls, for instance, it was argued, would no longer be able to drop science at 14, as many had tended to do in the past, as by continuing with the subject they would be able to take advantage of the opportunities created by local labour market shortages to work outside their traditional roles as well as within growing office and service occupations.

The requirement for every pupil to study a second language will, argue proponents of the vocational relevance of the National Curriculum, prepare new entrants to the workforce to compete in the open European market scheduled for 1992.

However, other subjects of direct vocational relevance, like careers education, have been elevated to the level of 'cross-curricular themes' which, like the place of computing in schools, are supposed to permeate every aspect of learning.

Other subjects with supposedly no vocational relevance, such as social studies, along with health and personal education, were dropped altogether. Home economics, an area of study that was overwhelmingly female in its teaching force and uptake, has also vanished. Yet it had over previous years transformed itself from a home-based concern with needlework and cookery to a wider interest in textiles, food and nutrition, as well as consumer issues, home management and preparation for parenthood.

Technology, which had similarly dragged itself out of the dark ages, when boys hammered away at woodwork, metalwork and technical drawing, to deal with design-solving in multi-materials, was preserved in the National Curriculum. Girls should now be able to participate in this area, and also in computing, even though computers still tend to be associated with mathematics rather than, as in most employment, with business or office practice. The latter, like home economics, is another stereotypically female option that has been lost from the National Curriculum.

These alternatives can still be accommodated, if schools wish, in the time left, apart from that allocated to the National Curriculum. However, they are no longer first priority, which is to fulfil the legal obligation to cover the prescribed subjects. These constitute a very traditional and academic approach to education, a factor which is clearly seen in the way subject boundaries are so rigidly defined.

The arbitrary limitation of subject boundaries in the National Curriculum is clearly seen in the case of the most directly vocationally relevant foundation subject of technology. In its broadest definition of applying intelligence to solve problems with practical implications, technology cannot be confined to a subject in itself. Yet its definition in the National Curriculum does just this by dropping the craft and design elements that were associated with technology's rebirth as CDT from woodwork, metalwork and technical drawing.

CDT, often grouped within schools in faculties including art and pottery, formed a bridge between scientific and aesthetic subjects. Its emphasis upon practical problem-solving potentially widened its application to all subjects. The working group devising the content of the redefined subject areas recognised that 'craft skills are the essential means to the achievement of many design goals'. They also urged consideration of the social and ecological consequences of technological decisions. They added a caution against a concentration on factual knowledge of technologies rather than their practical applications.

Yet rote learning of factual knowledge, when abstracted from its practical applications and social context, may be enhanced by the proposed tests at ages 7, 11, 14 and 16. These are at variance with what has become the accepted approach of open, child-centred, discovery learning in primary schools and, as will be seen, with student-centred approaches to negotiated, vocational curricula. They also duplicate but differ in approach from the new unitary GCSE examinations recently introduced into secondary schools. No other country has ever proposed such a framework of universal testing, although the enthusiasm of various states of the USA for ubiquitous school tests simple enough to be marked by computers is well known.

The new English measures hark back to the system of payment by results presented to Parliament in 1862, which ensured that the size of grants paid to schools related to the attainment of their pupils in tests conducted by the inspectors. The result was that teachers taught only to the tests, and the same situation may recur when publication of schools' test scores is made the basis of parental comparison between them. This 'consumer choice' may result, as the government intends, in the closure of the lowest scoring schools, thus saving on public expenditure.

Teachers rightly fear the confirmation of failure for those pupils performing below average in these tests; yet the whole profession has been drawn into assigning topics to levels, attainment targets and profile components. However sensitively they are applied, these tests cannot truly reflect pupils' abilities and talents; nor can they help supply the knowledge needed for employment in a rapidly changing social, technical, international and even natural environment.

The government has imposed uniform testing as a means of raising overall levels of attainment. Advocates of the reform argue this is the only way to raise Britain's deplorable standards of public education. Yet standards have risen considerably since the war: the number of school-leavers without any qualifications at all has dropped from about 70 to 10 per cent. 50 per cent left school in 1988 with one or more grade A to C GCSE, and 18 per cent with one or more A level.

This is not to suggest that examination results correlate in any direct way with individuals' performance at work, still less with the country's economic productivity. It merely shows that until recently standards have risen overall, irrespective of the type of school organisation – tripartite or comprehensive. Nor does it suggest there is no problem. Of all the industrialised countries, Britain retains among a substantial section of its population an aversion to education. Over the period 1978–88, although the population of 16-year-olds in full-time employment fell from 55 to 20 per cent, there was little corresponding rise in the proportion in full-time education. This passed 50 per cent for the first time only during 1988–89; but by the age of 18, the proportion in full-time education was still only 14 per cent. This compares with 80 per cent in the USA, Japan and Holland.

The desire of many British working-class youngsters to leave school at the earliest opportunity is deeply rooted. It also matches the expectations of many employers who do not recognise the value of extended education or training for their workers. Investment in training in the UK as a percentage of GNP is among the lowest in Europe. The aversion to education amongst so many of its workforce is likely to be increased by the academic approach of the National Curriculum.

From its inception, severe practical limitations have dogged the introduction of the National Curriculum. The chronic underfunding of education at all levels over many years, aggravated by repeated cuts during the late 1970s and early 1980s, means that most state schools lack basic equipment and even textbooks, whilst the state of school buildings has deteriorated to the extent of making many dangerous, if not unusable. There is also the chronic shortage of teachers caused primarily by the steady fall in the relative value of their wages. Shortages are particularly acute in the subjects which most directly apply to industry, where qualified teachers can gain more rewarding and better-paid posts.

The House of Commons Select Committee on Education in 1989 identified mathematics, chemistry, physics, modern languages and technology as specialisms in which teacher shortages will soon reach many thousands. Maths alone may lack 12,000 teachers by 1995 according to some forecasts. Two-thirds of the core curriculum is thus threatened at secondary level, along with much of the foundation.

In primary schools, where most teachers were not trained for subject specialisation, the situation is worse. In addition, primary pupil numbers are booming, unlike secondaries where numbers are (temporarily) falling. Teachers need more time to train: 10 per cent non-contact time was recommended by the Inspectorate for primary teachers, while teachers themselves demanded 20 per cent. Yet the whole new package has been rushed through at an impossible speed and is accompanied by many other distracting changes in the administration of the schools.

Thus time is at a premium, with understaffed and over-crowded schools forced to turn away pupils in some areas and to teach on a rota basis in others. Instead of raising teachers' pay, the government has tried to introduce non-qualified staff into schools by 'licensing' candidates for the profession whose only qualification will be the equivalent of C-grade passes in GCSE English and maths plus two years' higher education. This again can hardly produce the subject specialists who are required to deliver the National Curriculum. As HM Chief

Inspector said, 'without suitably qualified teachers, the rest falls'.

There is in any case nothing so new about the 'new' National Curriculum. For many years most secondary schools in England and Wales taught the same subjects at the same ages for the same examinations without any direct control by the central government, while in primary schools teachers, parents and pupils shared the objective of attaining functional literacy and numeracy, only the method of reaching that goal sometimes being in dispute.

What may be lost by introducing a prescribed curriculum for all pupils is the flexibility to respond to local circumstances and to draw upon the resources of the neighbourhood, including local industry, as some community schools and many vocational schemes attempted to do. What is gained in legislating for all pupils to follow the same subjects may not be much if, as seems likely, the new academic specifications turn out to be more of a notional than a National Curriculum.

The Technical and Vocational Education Initiative

So what is left of the government's previous enthusiasm for vocational education in schools? The Technical and Vocational Education Initiative which applies to all pupils in their last two years of secondary schooling is a survivor from 1983 when it launched its first fourteen pilot projects for 10,000 pupils.

TVEI embodied, in the words of a White Paper of the time, 'the government's policy that education should better equip young people for working life'. This was not to be achieved by raising standards of reading, writing and arithmetic through imposing upon all schools a National Curriculum based on a turn-of-the-century grammar school model. Instead, locally-based consortia of schools and FE colleges were to co-operate with their local industries to produce vocationally relevant courses for 14–18-year-olds.

The initiative was at first rejected by the schoolteachers and college lecturers involved. They saw it as a way to reintroduce selection into comprehensive schools. They predicted that TVEI would either create sink streams for those from whom little was expected, or cream off academic high-fliers for vocational technical courses. Their fears that this was an attempt to reinstate the tripartite system were not allayed by the announcement from the Employment Secretary, Norman Tebbit, that TVEI represented 'the rebirth of technical education'. His fellow government minister, Lord Young, even threatened the local education authorities that if they did not volunteer to run the initiative, the Department of Employment would set up its own schools to do so. He proposed calling these 'Young schools'! Given sufficient funding however the local authorities were soon falling over themselves to set up their own TVEI schemes, even though these were at this stage only supposed to be for selected pupils in certain schools.

TVEI did not develop as anyone predicted: there are now as many different TVEIs as there are schemes. A good illustration of what happened to one of the earliest pilots was in the West Midlands. The Black Country, once the heart of traditional 'metal-bashing' industry, suffered more than most as the recession deepened. By 1984, at Mons secondary school in the middle of a run-down Dudley housing estate, the majority of parents were out of work. Mons was proposed by the local education authority for inclusion in the TVEI consortium along with four other schools and the local further education college. The fact that needs in this area were so obviously greatest allayed the resentment in the authority's other schools at the cash injections the consortium would receive from the Manpower Services Commission.

A TVEI co-ordinator was then appointed in each school to liaise with MSC officials over how their extra £500,000 would be spent. At Mons the co-ordinator recalled, 'It was a pig's ear to start off with. Everything was in such a rush. The first bout of money was spent by advisers who then distanced themselves in case it went wrong, so the pilot ran itself basically.' Because of this the benefits were not restricted, as was originally intended, to selected streams within the schools but spread by teachers committed to comprehensive

21

education to all their fourth and fifth year pupils and later to all levels.

In fact, teachers soon began to use the money in their own ways to achieve what they had long wanted to do. In Mons' English department they bought computers to which all pupils could have access. One English teacher said,

> The great thing about TVEI was that it impressed upon management that we could have kids sitting around tables instead of in rows. They could do work in rough and produce a final version on wordprocessors, or work with felt pens on large sheets of paper to sketch out their ideas. Because the head's idea of English before that was doing spelling tests basically.
>
> As a result the school has been transformed. It was at the bottom of the authority's league table on every point. In fact, to say that it was a hell-hole would be an understatement. It was much worse than that! But now relationships have changed from very much 'them-and-us' because when TVEI introduced residential weeks away and allowed us the time for personal counselling on a one-to-one basis, staff actually had to start talking to students.

This teacher's verdict reflects the effects of five years of extra funding on one school in the Initiative. It has enabled the school to install computer terminals in every classroom and to begin networking with other schools in the consortium. A programme of in-service training for all staff has also given teachers the time to update or acquire their own computing skills. Information technology has thus become an integral part of every subject on the curriculum. It enables learning to be related across subject boundaries and offers opportunities for handling vast quantities of information in new ways completely different from the old rote learning of the past.

Craft, design and technology in particular has been transformed from traditional woodwork/metalwork to design and technology using new plastic materials. This mirrored some of the changes that were occurring in local industry, where some firms managed to incorporate traditional metal bashing into the wider context of plastic technologies. 'Now', as the school's careers teacher pointed out, 'kids leaving here know about vacuum forming or injection moulding, so when they see those jobs advertised they know what it involves.'

As the economy improved in the late 1980s, and although traditional jobs came back to some extent, school-leavers were less interested in them, partly because their own and their parents' faith in them as secure employment had been shaken. When in autumn 1988, the careers officer came to Mons school with information about engineering and construction apprenticeships, for the first time ever no one turned up to hear about them. Instead, many boys as well as girls now aim for employment in textiles, which have been introduced with new technology in some local firms. Caring professions in the service sector are also popular, as is shop work, another expanding area in Dudley, and pupils are introduced to all these occupations by TVEI modules of study, work experience and visits.

In some of the new service sectors there is no very clear career structure, even though the wages are reasonable at the outset. Yet more students have come to see the point of gaining better qualifications and of undertaking training. Exam results have improved and some of the school's greatest successes have been in getting girls into technical employment, which they would not have considered before.

'Of course', the TVEI co-ordinator conceded, 'you can't put all these changes down to TVEI. Partly it's the media. Nowadays everyone says they want to work in computers but they don't know what it means. In fact, very few people work exclusively at computing but more and more people work with computers whatever it is that they are doing.'

Nationally there has been a mixed evaluation of TVEI precisely because local schemes are so varied. Headteachers in TVEI schools were surveyed by the National Foundation for Educational Research, and while they welcomed the injections of extra cash they complained about the rush and confusion with which the Initiative had been launched upon them. Classroom teachers' perceptions were divided according to the extent to which they had been involved in the projects in their schools. This was another reason why heads sought to spread TVEI across departments, to prevent the resentments that would arise if any department were deprived of the extra funds.

Pupil judgements of the scheme depended upon whether it helped them in what they aimed to do, as well as whether it was inherently enjoyable. While not altering the aspirations of those pupils involved who intended to go on to A-level sixth form studies, only 17 per cent of the sample of other pupils remaining on TVEI after age 16 considered that it would help them get the job they wanted. However, the evaluation showed that the majority of students perceived the main benefits of TVEI to be related to increased self-confidence and their general abilities to solve practical problems, rather than to specific vocational skills. Another study showed that some parents considered TVEI to be academically inferior to other courses and were worried that their children would not be able to enter professional and white-collar careers if they followed the programme.

On its own terms, TVEI failed to retain the majority of its pupils for a 14–18 in-school complement to YTS, as was originally planned. Numbers of pupils who decided to stay on after the school-leaving age to complete the course varied from one local authority to another and even from school to school. In Birmingham, for example, 65 per cent of pupils stayed on in 1985, while in neighbouring Sandwell the figure was only 26 per cent. Birmingham was unrepresentative both because the collapse of job opportunities was particularly rapid in the city that year and because YTS enjoyed an especially poor reputation there. Since then, the extension of TVEI in 1986 to all pupils has made these comparisons unnecessary.

This expansion, while it promised an additional £900 million to the £200 million already spent on piloting TVEI, disbursed the additional money over ten years and to all secondary schools, so causing TVEI's influence to extend further but to be spread more thinly. The National Union of Teachers calculated that it represented a drop in expenditure from £600 to only £150 per pupil and was sufficient only to supply three-quarters of an extra technical teacher to each school.

TVEI had signally failed in one of its initial objectives of involving employers in the funding of technical training in schools. It was supposed to be a 'pump-priming' exercise and, once government funding had demonstrated the virtues of the pilot scheme, employers were intended to put up their own money to fund its virtues. This has not happened. Despite their declared enthusiasm for the Initiative and many of the government's other vocational efforts, employers continue to show a stubborn resistance to actually parting with hard-earned cash in order to invest in education. They do not regard this as their responsibility and can see no prospects of any immediate returns on the investments they are asked to make. The same was to happen when the City Technology Colleges succeeded TVEI as the government's next and last major vocational initiative in schools.

In addition, TVEI has been all but forgotten in the latest education reforms, despite policy statements welcoming the achievements of the initial pilot schemes. These, the Department of Education and Science declared in 1985, 'are laying a foundation which we must build on' to bring 'a more relevant and practical curriculum' to 'all young people in school'. In the same year the White Paper *Better Schools* promoted TVEI as the prototype for future education reform. The Department of Employment endorsed this verdict in its White Paper on education and training in 1986 which announced the extension to a national scheme. 'The objective will be to give young people aged 14–18 in all maintained schools and colleges access to a wider and richer curriculum based on the lessons emerging from the pilot TVEI project.'

Just one year later in a government consultation document on the National Curriculum, the long paragraphs extolling the virtues of the Initiative were reduced to only two passing mentions. Since then the whole purpose of TVEI has been redefined into one of merely supporting the National Curriculum. When its funding ends in 1996 the whole scheme may be officially forgotten.

Back in Dudley the pilot schools are already looking forward to life after TVEI. The extension funds have been channelled to the other schools in the authority which had not previously benefited from TVEI's largess. The consortium schools have continued to collaborate in appealing to local employers to advance technical and academic co-operation. Together they have employed a public relations firm to make a promotional video aimed at employers to attract cash sponsorship. But whether sufficient funding can be found from local firms is doubtful, although the fall in school rolls has made some employers more anxious to secure the new employees they require by becoming more involved in schools at earlier stages. It is not factory fodder they are seeking but school-leavers who are able to react flexibly to changing conditions. While this may be seen as a demand for semi-skilled labour, it is also true that new technology makes increasing demands upon at least some employees and that pupils were prepared for this through using new technology on TVEI. However, another effect of falling rolls has been to close one of the schools in the Dudley TVEI pilot consortium, while the headteacher of another was at one time talking about opting out to save his school.

Such division was predicted by critics who saw TVEI only as a means to take over the comprehensive school curriculum and its local control by teachers and education authorities. Now that this has been achieved by direct central government legislation, which also encourages the setting up of separate City Technology Colleges and opted-out direct grant grammar schools, they would argue that there is less need to concentrate on initiatives designed to promote differentiation within schools.

However, it is also true that, as Anne Jones, the head of education programmes at the Training Agency (MSC as was), pointed out in 1987, 'Teachers have taken control of the Technical and Vocational Education Initiative and moulded it to suit their pupils' needs'. A deputy head of one of the Dudley TVEI consortium schools was confident that whether or not their appeal for funds was successful, the initiative had made a permanent change for the better in education in the area.

'That's the whole success of TVEI in this school', he asserted. 'It's not going to go away just because the money has finished. It's built into the bricks and mortar of the place. It hasn't just fizzled out like so much educational practice which has launched so many advisers on their careers and that's the end of it.'

Of course more money would obviously help. There will no longer be any residential component to the course and the school cannot proceed with the computer building that it planned to enable all GCSE project work to be word-processed. As the deputy head says,

> We want to be a 'high tech' school and the government know what a 'high tech' school costs because they have just spent £7 million on Solihull City Technology College. But we could do it better with only the £1 million that industry put into it above the £6 million from the taxpayer.
>
> Every day I drive past that building on my way to work and I am so bitter about the fact that they can spend so much on one school I can hardly talk about it. Somebody called it a cheap political stunt but I call it an expensive political stunt. The damage it is doing to teacher morale cannot be underestimated.

City Technology Colleges

The first three City Technology Colleges were opened in 1988 and 1989. The first was Kingshurst CTC in Solihull, which aroused such strong feelings of anger and resentment in the neighbouring Dudley's deputy headteacher. CTCs have provoked similar resistance everywhere they have been proposed. Because of this the original plan for them has proved impossible to achieve and in 1989 the Secretary of State announced that extra finance for buildings would be terminated after the first twenty colleges had been built.

The plan for twenty 'beacons of excellence', 'halfway houses between the independent and state sectors', to open by 1990 was revealed to a standing ovation from the 1986 Conservative Party Conference. In reality, fewer than half that number would be opened by 1990, of which only one was in one of the 27 inner-city areas originally designated in the glossy prospectus for the initiative. Neither were they financed 'wholly or substantially' by industry, with government funding their day-to-day running costs, as was also the declared intention. Instead, private industrialists promised to contribute about a quarter of the start-up costs, leaving the government to find about £140,000,000. A ministerial answer to a question in the House of Commons on 14 November 1989 gave the government's planned expenditure on CTCs by the end of 1991–92 as £122.3 million, compared with £43 million pledged by business and industry.

Neither were CTCs to be non-selective schools in inner city areas, as was proposed. Local authorities in those areas trying to close or amalgamate schools to cope with falling rolls did not welcome new schools beyond their control which would attract their most highly motivated children. So all but two of the scheduled CTCs had to relocate to the suburbs.

Church authorities proved more amenable to converting their existing schools to CTCs or starting up new ones in their old premises. In return, however, they forced changes in order to allow the establishment of denominational technology colleges, including one for born-again Christians, funded incidentally by a local car salesman! There are also such anomalies as a City College for the Performing Arts (another new invention) which is sited adjacent to a second CTC in Croydon, both within 15 miles of one of the other scheduled CTCs.

However, numbers do not matter, say their supporters. No-one has ever suggested that just twenty schools for between 750 and 1,000 pupils each could begin to answer Britain's training needs. It is the example which the CTCs provide to other schools that is important, but it has not impressed some of Britain's leading industrialists. The Director of the Industrial Society said the Department of Education and Science was 'living in a fantasy world' if it expected industry to provide the £5 or £6 million for each college. He argued that instead of establishing new schools 'the government should be putting its efforts into encouraging companies to improve the quality of their existing links with inner city schools'.

John Harvey-Jones, former Chairman of ICI, voiced his opinion on BBC's *Panorama* that CTCs are an inefficient way for industry to invest in education. His company spurned government requests to sponsor a CTC near one of its largest plants in Cleveland, although it invests £5 million annually in other educational projects. Other big companies with educational interests, like BP, also declined to be involved.

Of 1,800 firms initially approached by the CTC Trust set up to lobby for the new schools, only 17 responded positively. The sponsors who eventually came forward fall, according to *Labour Research*, into four overlapping categories: 'companies which make donations to the Conservatives and other right-wing parties; rich individuals; property developers; and medieval livery companies in the City of London'. Many of the latter already sustain private schools in various parts of the country.

What the CTC proposal represented at the time of its announcement was a bridge between the previous policy of vocational education and the new education reforms which were then being devised. By concentrating all resources into a few inner-city centres, they were an admission that the effort to bring vocational education to all schools was too expensive to continue without the private employer funding which had not been forthcoming.

At the same time the CTCs presented a model for the way to run schools which opted out from local authority control. Set up as limited companies, they would be controlled by boards of governors and funded on a *per capita* basis from central government for every pupil they managed to attract. They would be able to stay open for a longer school day, have shorter holidays and pay their staff at different rates from other state schools.

Nottingham CTC's staff contract stipulates that employees cannot belong to any trade union which has not renounced the right to strike. Eventually all schools might follow this model under their own financial management. The prototype was in turn taken from the method used by the Manpower Services Commission to fund the private training agencies which provided its youth and other training programmes.

CTCs have therefore clearly already had a considerable influence, but what do they offer as far as vocational education is concerned? Their curriculum was drawn up by consultants from the Organisation for Rehabilitation and Training (ORT). This Israeli-based charity began in Tsarist Russia training unemployed Zionist youth. Its approach is narrowly utilitarian and its trade schools in France seem the inspiration for many of the government's efforts during the vocational phase of its education policy.

ORT's recommendations for the CTCs included sorting pupils on the basis of its own aptitude tests into 'advanced', 'mainstream' and 'vocational' streams and replacing lessons with 'educational events'. The principal of Kingshurst, Valerie Bragg, said she ignored this advice. However, Kingshurst speaks its own language of 'learning parameters and procedures' under different 'area managers' (i.e. heads of department). Even the school-keeper at Nottingham CTC is known as 'the site engineer'! Blackboards have also been banned, but for the sensible practical reason that chalk would clog up all the new electronic equipment with which the building bristles. The modern office decor of Kingshurst CTC is easily imagined, with undisguised overhead ducting, plastic worktops, and carpet tastefully selected by the principal to match the pupils' uniforms. Every room has its own television, telephone, video and satellite link, and desktop computers are available on a one-to-one basis. Pupils are registered and relentlessly tested and retested on computer programmes. Significantly, the library is the least well-stocked part of the school.

CTCs are exempt from the provisions of the National Curriculum but Kingshurst's timetable for the first-year intake is not so different from that offered in many comprehensives, especially those building upon TVEI: three hours of maths, English and science a week, two hours of CDT, food technology and French, with one hour each for information processing, music, drama and business economics, plus options in programming or foreign cookery. The stress which the principal places upon the humanities and self-expression – 'Industry does not want robots', she says – increases Kingshurst's resemblance to an ordinary non-technical secondary school. Her staff emphasise group work and technology across the curriculum so that it infuses all subjects and is not an activity in itself. This also follows best practice in other state schools.

Developing business enterprise is something they are particularly keen on at Kingshurst. Frequent projects take over and integrate with the usual timetable to form mini-businesses which market their products. These exercises too are not peculiar to Kingshurst CTC and have been performed in many primary schools. What is different of course are the facilities, and the equipment available to follow this curriculum. For physical education, for instance, a lavishly equipped multigym is available as an option to all pupils.

The school is also very definitely selective, although it claims not to be. One of its proudest of many computer demonstrations is of the bell-curve of its pupils' achievement in the IQ test they take on entry. This statistically even distribution across the ability range is disputed by other local schools. They show the test results in mathematics and verbal reasoning attained in their last term at primary school by Kingshurst entrants were 11 and 12 points higher than those pupils admitted to other schools.

Indeed, one of the government's Education Ministers, Angela Rumbold, admitted that 'With the most highly-motivated pupils out of the way, teachers in the other schools will be able to concentrate on the broad band of pupils who are fairly well motivated'.

For it is motivation that is the crucial element in learning. Selection from the 350 applicants for Kingshurst's 180 first-year places was made on the basis of an interview with parents and child where motivation was the deciding factor. Children had to be prepared to undertake the longer hours and greater amount of homework than would be expected elsewhere, and to agree that they would remain at the school until age 18.

Other schools in Solihull were threatened with closure by Kingshurst's opening. 'It is no coincidence', said the head-teacher of nearby and now closed Simon Digby school, 'that the CTC opened in September and we're talking about closing in October.' Nor is it a coincidence that the first CTC opened in the Conservative-controlled authority which had pre-viously tried to reintroduce grammar schools against parental opposition. Labour councillors who had successfully cam-paigned against that attempt to reintroduce selection had argued instead for a tertiary college in North Solihull. This would, they claimed, have provided opportunities for children on the large, working-class estates whom the CTC is now so proud of helping.

It is not possible that all children can benefit from the example of these few schools catering for a select group of pupils in specific areas of the country. Nor can it seem a very realistic example to follow for schools in Nottingham, for example, where £9.05 million was spent in building one new school, compared with the city's entire annual capital spend-ing on all its schools of less than £2.5 million. As the head-teacher of a neighbouring Solihull comprehensive com-plained, 'Kingshurst CTC is funded on a scale never seen in my school. Inevitably it will draw away from my school some of the best pupils and, perhaps, some of the best teachers. Then the CTC will say to my school – we must compete with each other.'

Such bitter feelings made it unlikely that local education authorities would take seriously the offers of co-operation with their schools that the CTCs have started to make. So, although CTCs may be forced into supplying hi-tech training for local companies and other extra activities, including good works for the unemployed on Employment Training, it is unlikely that they can go the way of TVEI to integrate with comprehensive provision. Nor is their proposed transform-ation into less expensive 'magnet schools', specialising on an American model in one particular subject, likely to ingratiate them with other local schools. The CTCs' co-operation with opted-out schools and with CDT departments in private schools to provide selective technical training make integration even more unlikely.

The CTC programme was closely identified with the Education Secretary of the time at which they were established, Kenneth Baker. Although his successor remains officially committed to it, CTCs have served their purpose for government and many would like to see them quietly forgotten, especially as they are so expensive: the government spent £33 million on its three CTCs in 1989, more than it set aside for the introduction that year of the National Curriculum into all 30,000 schools in the country. It would cost £2.8 billion to equip every secondary school in England and Wales to the same standard as Kingshurst CTC in Solihull. Since no government would ever spend so much extra on education it is idle to pretend that the CTCs have anything to do with raising standards in general or vocational education in particular. It is the dishonesty of this irrelevant and scandalously political gesture that has aroused such opposition to it.

Rather than continue negative criticism of something which has nothing to do with education and training, it is better to pass on to analysis of something which does.

Youth Training

The Youth Training Scheme was introduced in an attempt to make a virtue out of necessity. The intention behind its launch in 1983 was to use the national tragedy of mass youth unemployment as an opportunity to establish for the first time a permanent programme of integrated education and training for all school leavers, employed and unemployed alike.

YTS succeeded the main temporary make-work programme for unemployed youth, the Youth Opportunities Programme, with what was intended to be a modernised apprenticeship for everybody. Its one-year programme of on-the-job training would replace old time-served apprenticeships. Instead of three or four years of narrow craft specialisation, YTS would offer foundation training in one of the eleven occupational training families into which the MSC divided every possible occupation in the economy. The second year, which was added to the scheme in 1986, was supposed to build upon these foundation skills acquired in the first year by deepening them in practical application within a particular occupational area, even though this reintroduced an element of time-serving to the scheme.

YTS has established itself as a permanent addition to the training landscape and been built into many firms' recruitment practices, but the scheme has failed in its ambitious aims, partly for structural and partly for contingent reasons. Most fundamentally, YTS was never a universal scheme for all young people. It was always a programme for working-class youth. It aimed to replace apprenticeships which, almost by definition, had been virtually restricted to young, working-class men. One inspiration of YTS, as far as many involved in its formulation and implementation were concerned, was to open up to all young people the new apprenticeship system which developments in technology made possible. This remains the intention behind the effort to standardise and relate all vocational and professional qualifications so as to enable progression and transfer between them (see the section on National Vocational Qualifications, page 70).

It was hoped that YTS to age 18 would complement developments in schools and colleges. Even if the 'old sixth formers' continued to follow an academic route to higher education, it was anticipated that there would be 'new sixth formers' remaining in education because they were unemployed. They would undertake vocational education to age 18, either on TVEI or by following other work-related courses leading to the Certificate of Pre-Vocational Education. CPVE, according to the original plan, would also certify YTS completion. Except for the Northern Irish Youth Training Plan, introduced one year earlier than YTS, this did not happen.

YTS did not succeed in raising the age of selection for future destination in society, or rather its confirmation, beyond the school-leaving age at 16. Selection for the great divide in the working population between those who work with their hands and those who work with their brains continues to be made within the schools. This tendency can only be confirmed by the reintroduction of an academic National Curriculum. Unlike the schools, however, YT cannot even pretend to offer equal opportunities to all. It is restricted to the non-academics who do not continue their education. The route to professional occupations is effectively closed by joining most YT.

Although wages in many trades surpass those of many increasingly proletarianised professions, manual workers, and also those in routine office and service non-manual occupations, do not enjoy parity of esteem with the non-manual professions. Furthermore, there are not usually the same opportunities for career progression in manual and routine non-manual occupations.

Restricted at the outset to working-class school-leavers (almost synonymous terms), YTS also failed to include all of them, yet it was supposed to be for employed and unemployed alike. The Manpower Services Commission protested that 'YTS is first and last a training scheme and not about youth unemployment'. Yet in its first year the proportion of employed trainees anticipated was revised downwards from 33 per cent to only 5 per cent.

Later the Scheme guaranteed a place only to the unemployed but, since the 1988 withdrawal of benefit rights to those under 18 (with very few exceptions), this 'guarantee' is all too often in the nature of an offer which cannot be refused. This element of compulsion existed from very early on: in 1984–85 11,000 youngsters had benefit cut for leaving schemes and 2,000 suffered the same fate for refusing to join them.

The association of the training scheme with unemployment and the make-work programmes that had preceded it doomed YTS to a second-rate status. It quickly became confirmed as a last resort for many youngsters who could find no other alternative. This low status for YTS was enhanced by the speed with which the scheme was hurriedly cobbled together and the constant pressure to get results as cheaply as possible. Many of the programmes were so badly organised initially that one participant in them wrote, 'they succeeded, not in introducing young people to the world of work, but rather to a world of constant confusion'. The new brand of small entrepreneurs entrusted by the MSC with the delivery of many schemes became notorious for the specious claims of their advertising and the poor quality of their training.

It says much for the forbearance of working-class parents that they entrusted their youngsters to such a scheme. For several years it had in most cases no clearly defined objectives, no recognised certification and no common and agreed means of attaining its ends beyond the work experience all trainees were expected to undertake, if even that could be found for them. It is hardly imaginable that middle-class parents would enter their offspring for any similarly ill-defined course of academic study at schools, or that teachers would be allowed to foist such a hodgepodge upon them.

Most working-class youngsters had no other choice, but they did protest against the threat of compulsion to YTS which was announced in 1985. This marked the largest school-student strike in British history, when a quarter-of-a-million pupils walked out of schools to march in towns and cities throughout the country. Trainees mostly voted with their feet. Completion rates were low and chronic scheme-changing replaced the switching around by those who did not gain or keep an apprenticeship between similar, tedious 'dead-end' jobs in the past.

An obvious cause of dissatisfaction is the low level of the YT allowance. Its value has constantly fallen, even in comparison with YOP, which paid the equivalent of £40 a week in comparison with the first-year YTS allowance. This was only fixed at £27.50 after protests against the government's original proposal of £15. The 1989–90 rate of £29.50 in the first year and £35 in the second represents benefit levels for those under 18.

Because they are not employees, Youth Trainees do not share the same rights to employment protection which exist for other workers. Nor are they covered by much of the Race Relations and Sex Discrimination Acts, while the health and safety record of the scheme has been appalling. There has been a growing rate of fatal and major accidents since 1985 to 132.2 per 100,000 (compared with 90 for all employees).

Yet the research reports of all interviews with Youth Trainees show that, like students, they would be prepared to put up with a paltry allowance, if not poor conditions, so long as they knew their efforts would be rewarded by proper training leading to good employment prospects. Unfortunately this is not always the case, especially in areas of high unemployment.

The criterion for success set for YTS was how many of its trainees would manage to secure employment at the end of it. Yet for many young people entry to YTS became the first step, not to getting a job, but to a whole series of government schemes. On Merseyside and in the North East, people still graduate from YT to Employment Training and other adult programmes without ever having a proper job.

Research also indicates that joining YT can confirm a young person's unemployed and, eventually, unemployable, status. Hence many youngsters avoid the scheme and try to get 'a proper job' of any sort, even one without prospects of further training or progression. Yet if they forgo entry to YT, they may have missed their only chance to get training of any sort.

When it was first introduced, YTS actually contributed to the unemployment it was supposed to alleviate. This was confirmed by the Auditor General's report, *Vocational Education and Training for Young People*, in 1985. Job substitution replaced permanent adult employees with temporary young trainees. It was endorsed by 'additionality', by which government paid employers to add five trainees to their workforce in place of two young workers. This further ensured a degrading competition between the five trainees for the two jobs that might or might not be available at the end of the year.

There has always been a temptation for employers to use

the scheme to acquire cheap labour. The first major survey of employers' relations to YTS found that 'The most important advantage to employers participating in the YTS is the opportunity it gives them to look at or screen young people before offering permanent employment. Also important are the savings that result on labour costs.' By subsidising employers who give young people menial tasks and then return them to the dole queue, YOP/YTS increased employers' reliance upon state funds to use temporary trainees whom they did not have to train.

These abuses were all in the initial days of the scheme, argue its proponents. They have now been overcome along with other teething problems. However, while there have been some improvements, YT is still marked by what was supposed to be its main virtue of being employer-led. This 'responsiveness to market forces' merely reflects and reinforces the existing segregation of labour by race and gender. Thus, despite fine words on equal opportunities, the scheme has not been able to confront racism and sexism but serves to institutionalise existing divisions in the labour market and to perpetuate inequalities. There have been repeated complaints that YT relegates black youth to schemes from which there is less likelihood of leaving for employment. Young women meanwhile continue to be over-represented on schemes training for low-paid, traditionally feminine work.

The result of following the labour market was that a clear hierarchy of YT quickly emerged. At the top of the pile are schemes guaranteeing employment in large companies and subject only to trainees' attaining minimum levels of performance. These are mainly apprenticeships brought within the scheme and the YT allowance paid to the trainee by the government is often topped up by the employer to the old apprenticeship rate. Since their trainees are classified as apprentices, these schemes are only nominally a part of YT; entry is highly selective and those lucky enough to get in enjoy better training on the job plus more instruction off it.

Next come schemes offering training if not jobs in occupationally-specific skills which are in demand in the local labour market. These skills are certified by the colleges or other agents running them in ways that are credible to future employers. While they do not guarantee access to better than averagely paid, semi-skilled work, they offer a fair chance.

Other schemes offer no certainty of acquiring marketable skills nor of gaining employment. Employers, mostly small firms, use them mainly to screen potential recruits should vacancies arise. Here, placements are in non-unionised, low-paying firms but at least there is some chance of employment.

On other schemes, run mostly by private managing agents, there is no chance of employment at all. They are totally detached from the processes of selection and recruitment to labour. These were what were known as 'Mode B' schemes for disabled and 'disadvantaged' youth. They include schemes run on employers' premises but run largely as an expression of social responsibility. Here, as one researcher found, 'the additional "goats" are from the start distinguished from the "sheep" who comprise the normal intake'. Because Mode B schemes unsurprisingly did little to enhance their trainees' job prospects, they were abandoned in 1986. All YT is now supposed to be based in employment.

Interim guidance from the Department of Employment to the local employers on the Training and Enterprise Councils, which since 29 May 1990 run YT in their areas, show the same distinctions resurfacing in the form of those young people designated as having 'special training needs'. They will be identified by the Careers Service, which will then place them in one of three categories: A, requiring Initial Training for up to six months; B, those who will not realistically achieve a level 2 National Vocational Qualification; C, those who will achieve such an NVQ only with additional help. However, it is not clear how the quality of the TECs' special training needs provision in YT will be monitored and evaluated (if at all).

YT schemes thus fall into two basic categories: those which place primary emphasis on trainees gaining a qualification and those where the main aim will be to get trainees quickly into jobs. The former trainees will be worth investing in to the level of NVQ levels 3 or 4 (equivalent to craft and technician levels respectively). The latter may need help to reach level 2 but if they have 'still not found employment by the age of 17.5 years he/she is to be offered intensive job search and tasting or training in enterprise and self-employment'.

The divisions in YT following the pre-existing divisions in the labour market have been accentuated by the partial recovery of the economy which has occurred in parts of the country since the YTS was first introduced. Uptake of YT reflects local labour market conditions: where the economy is buoyant YT has become an irrelevance. In London and the South East many employers, especially small firms, have gone back to their traditional methods of recruitment by word of mouth and informal training on the job, even if they are still subsidised by YT, while many large employers have formally opted-out of the scheme. Even in Sheffield the large council-run and subsidised scheme has now more or less collapsed.

Many other employers, despite the cheap labour it offered them, always preferred their traditional ways, rather than become involved in YTS and entangled in its bureaucracy. Another factor discouraging the establishment of national training standards is the government's encouragement of regional and even plant bargaining of wages and conditions.

Although about a quarter of 16-year-olds nationwide enter the scheme (28 per cent of boys and 24 per cent of girls – 1988 figures), in parts of the North the majority do so. For them the gap has widened between schemes guaranteeing secure employment, or at least improving chances of gaining it, and schemes of last resort into which youngsters are forced if they are unemployed. The attempt at creating a coherent, national programme of training whilst simultaneously occupying the young unemployed has thus split into what were always its two parts. Responsibility for training has been taken away from a national co-ordinating body (the Manpower Services Commission used to perform this role). Now local Training and Enterprise Councils, largely made up of local employers, decide what government-sponsored training goes on in their areas. Yet employers have never taken responsibility for training in the past.

What is likely is that, as with the Private Industry Councils in the USA upon which TECs are modelled, employers may encourage only the training that they require. The rest of YT may drift towards state-run 'workfare', forcing people into jobs at any cost. Employers will be reluctant to pay for this, especially as TEC funding by government was cut soon after TECs were set up. Spending on YT was also cut from £1,010 million in 1989–90 to £763 million in 1992–93, a drop from £50 per week per trainee to £33 per week.

Like the CTCs and TVEI, with which it was once intended to co-ordinate, YTS for 16–18-year-olds was supposed to be a pump-priming exercise. Employers, seeing how good it was in practice, would support it with their own cash. When YTS was lengthened to two years in 1986, it was optimistically assumed in the 1985 budget that employers would pay for the second year. Unfortunately, this has not happened.

YT no longer even pretends to present itself as a coherent national programme. Entitlement is no longer to a two-year training programme but to a level of training (NVQ level 1 or 2 in one case, level 3 or 4 in the other). 'Training will last for a stated period which is reasonable', says an introduction to YT. There may also be 'part-time YT'. Training providers no longer have to follow the old YTS design framework but are 'free to adapt patterns and mixes of training and methods of trainee assessment best suited to the . . . particular circumstances'. Similarly, the age limit is raised from 18 to 25, in line with the lower rates of benefit paid to under-25-year-olds since April 1988. Nor are there any longer any formal limits to the duration of YT programmes. The collapse of two-year YTS coincided with the simultaneous abandonment of the attempt to create a vocational education in schools. Instead, a traditional, academic National Curriculum has been imposed upon them which has little or no vocational relevance.

The disappointing outcome of all the effort that went into YTS is a result of another of the fundamental structural weaknesses of the scheme. It offered foundation training to all entrants to encourage flexibility and adaptability across a range of occupations. Employers increasingly require this type of labour for work which the introduction of new technology in many occupations within companies and in different firms in various manufacturing and commercial areas has rendered more similar. Employers are however reluctant to pay for such generalised training precisely because it is applicable in so many different areas. They will invest in training only for the few jobs that are still occupationally specific, and where they can get a substantial return on their investment in time and money before the employee is 'poached' by another employer.

Employers do not see why they should be involved in training for generalised skills, such as the computer literacy or keyboard familiarity which was supposed to be a component part of every YTS course, any more than they should be responsible for the functional literacy and numeracy which is supposed to be instilled by the schools. But as the government was reluctant to invest in education in order to provide the new pre-vocational skills increasingly required of all workers, it attempted to save money by creating a new semi-private training sector administered by the state through the Manpower Services Commission. This also tried to combine training with maintaining the work ethic of the unemployed, and was widely seen as a way of keeping them off the streets. When unemployment fell, especially in the younger age range (primarily because of demographic rather than economic changes), the national training effort collapsed. After a decade of spending billions of pounds on training we are back to square one, with employers crying out because of skill shortages and with no real improvement in the skills base of the workforce.

Although this may seem an almost totally negative assessment of YT, it is a realistic overview, even if there are obviously wide variations within it. Good Youth Training schemes can be found, offering training with recognised qualifications and opportunities for future employment. For instance, the 176 Information Technology Centres training 12,500 trainees were set up as the CTCs of YTS. They were often described as 'the jewel in the crown' of a locality's YTS provision. They certainly provide adequate training for the 90 per cent of their trainees who gain qualifications sufficient to get a start as information technicians, often in less time than was required under the YTS time-serving conditions.

Yet, like CTCs, ITeCs demonstrate the problems of putting all your computers in one basket. For the ITeCs are prevented from collaborating with schools, colleges and other schemes because their funding has been cut and they are expensive to run, let alone continuously update their equipment. They are therefore under continuous pressure to commercialise and sell their training and employment services. By servicing employed-status YT, branching out into consultancy and higher-level in-house staff training, as well as retraining women returning to work after having a family, the ITeCs are managing to survive as part of Youth Training, just.

From young people's point of view the acid test for any Youth Training scheme is whether it has increased access to occupations they would not have been able to enter before, and in some schemes this has been the case. British Rail, for example, always used to restrict entry into its traffic division to those over 18, largely because of the hours of work involved. Even though its trainees are expected to work from between six in the morning to ten at night, BR's employed-status YT offers access to a middle range of employment that was previously closed to young people. Trainees are rotated through a series of jobs including catering, passenger station operations, timetables and signals. Like management trainees whom many retail firms begin by placing for short periods in all positions in their outlets, BR's trainees become familiar with all the aspects of the divison's work. There are subsequent prospects of career progression to supervisory and more specialised levels. In fact, the scheme was introduced by management partly as a way of introducing some career stability to railway work which, even during periods of high unemployment, had suffered a high turnover of staff.

Another instance of YT creating opportunities for young

people where none existed before is chartered surveying. This was a graduate-only profession but many of the graduates employed typically underused the knowledge acquired on their university courses. There was thus room for an intermediate level, equivalent to level 3 or 4 of the National Vocational Qualification, with a traineeship that was similar to an apprenticeship, but to a professional occupation. It is thus possible in this case that graduate-level employees have been replaced by YT-trained multi-skilled operatives. However, surveying is such a booming business, even during periods of general recession, that it can never get all the graduate entrants it requires.

To take another example, in the case of video servicing, YTS-trained school-leavers took over more routine tasks from graduate electricians. It is quite possible however that those graduates also found more demanding work by using their training elsewhere. There are so many factors at work that it is difficult to determine what is happening to skill levels in any given industry. New technology requires higher skills at some levels even while it de-skills by simplifying at other levels.

In general however, YT comes a poor third for 16-year-old school-leavers to paid employment with guaranteed training and further progression, or to college courses. Further education can provide the same training on student conditions with the benefits of shorter hours and longer holidays, if not with adequate subsistence.

The experience of attempting to introduce for the first time a national training scheme for all young people is not all negative, however, as it has shown what is required if the skills needed to use the new technology to its fullest extent are ever to be available to everyone.

Compacts

If YT attempts to meet employers' demands for training for school-leavers, what are the demands that employers make of schools? Characteristically they are couched in very broad and general terms, as 'pupils should have the ability to learn how to learn' or 'to think for themselves and act independently'. Usually such abilities are judged initially by examination results, followed by suitable dress for and appropriate answers at interviews. Regular attendance, punctuality and positive attitudes may also be confirmed by school reports.

Some employers state that it is important their employees know 'how to work as members of a team'. For many jobs employees are sought who can 'take responsibility' and 'use their own initiative'. To encourage the same non-specific attributes some firms send their managers on 'adventure-training' courses of the Outward Bound type also attended by trainees on some YTS and TVEI programmes.

Some surveys of employers' requirements from school-leavers include a demand for specific records of a pupil's actual and potential achievements in school, hence the development of records of achievement which detail many of the pupils' activities in school. For most job applications, however, it is examination grades that are the indicators used to screen applicants for interviews. Since employers select from the top down, it is not surprising that many end up with employees who are overqualified for the work they are asked to perform. A record of achievement may be valuable, however, if only for giving interviewee and interviewer something to talk about.

Interviews are crucial for employment selection despite their notorious unreliability for predicting subsequent job performance. Interviewers characteristically make up their minds about a candidate within the first four minutes of an interview and rarely change their opinion thereafter. Non-verbal behaviour by candidates often plays a larger part in determining their success than their experience or qualifications. Interviewers typically assess a candidate on only two or three criteria, even when they are expected to assess against nine or ten, and they are more likely to be swayed by negative than by positive information or behaviour by the candidate. They also frequently rate male candidates higher than female and are generally more sympathetic to their own sex. The ratings of a candidate can even be affected by whether they follow another candidate who rated either very high or very low; thus the sequence of interviews exercises an arbitrary influence on the outcome.

These are only some of the findings of research into recruitment interviews, not to mention the effects of interviewer-bias due to racial stereotyping and discrimination against the disabled. Yet employers persist with interviews because they believe they are skilled and experienced enough to spot the right candidate.

Employers do not as a rule ask schools to provide them with specific skills related to particular occupations beyond, say, some keyboard facility for office employment. Specific skills can be developed on the job or through specialised training for which the employee will first have shown an aptitude and interest. In any case, such job-specific skills are becoming rarer. With the application of new technology to nearly all employment in industry and commerce, 'computer literacy' is becoming as important as was functional numeracy and literacy in the first Industrial Revolution.

The need for a workforce that could count and take measurements, follow written instructions and fill in forms and invoices was one reason why Victorian employers overcame their initial reluctance to allow their workers' children to be educated in state schools. A few mill and factory owners made pioneering efforts to educate their own employees in factory schools, but the majority of employers who eventually came around to supporting the introduction of elementary education to state schools did not volunteer to supply this education themselves. They considered it was the state's duty to provide it.

Similarly today, schools are expected to familiarise all young people from the earliest age with the computers now used throughout industry, but at much greater expense than the chalks and slates of old. A start has been made by providing an average 2.5 computers in each primary school and 23.2 in secondaries. According to the Department of Education and Science figures for 1988, the majority of primary pupils in all age groups had some hands-on experience of computers, as had three-quarters of secondary school pupils.

Apart from computer studies, a subject which current best practice indicates should be spread across all subjects, computers are mainly used as wordprocessors in business studies, or for modelling and design work in craft, design and technology, and with synthesisers for composition in music. Still, the average primary school spends only £500 a year on computers, while the average secondary school spends £5,000. HM Inspectors consider that computers are not always used by schools to their fullest potential. Indeed if they were, and every child had regular access to a machine to use in every subject, computers would, the Inspectors predict, 'transform the classroom as they have radically changed the home and workplace'.

Chalk and talk is much cheaper and less challenging to received ideas and ways of doing things, and this traditional model of imparting predefined knowledge has been reinstated by the National Curriculum. Teachers may be forced back towards communicating to serried ranks of pupils 'the facts' necessary to pass the tests that indicate assimilation of discrete subject knowledge. Group and team work, individual exploration and the interrelating of various facets of knowledge one to another may be squeezed out, even though these activities encourage precisely those qualities that employers say they look for in their new employees. Similarly, expensive new technology is concentrated in selective institutions like the City Technology Colleges, rather than being shared amongst all who need access to it.

Yet at the same time that these changes are being introduced into schools, some employers are becoming so desperate to secure their future labour supplies in the face of a falling youth population that they are prepared to become involved in the schools, often for the first time. As a result, some companies have linked up with schools in their area to form 'school–industry compacts'. These are often connected to urban renewal programmes in the larger cities, where previously big city-centre employers had relied upon recruiting

from the suburbs rather than from their immediately surrounding inner-city ghettos.

This is the model of Compact drawn from Boston in America, where a largely black inner-city population was being
left out of the economic redevelopment (what Governor
Dukakis used to call 'the Massachusetts miracle') which was
overtaking the central city area, while new businesses were
importing labour from outside the state. A judicial enquiry
had revealed that Boston's high juvenile crime rate was
largely attributable to pupils and ex-pupils from two or three
schools, while the overall high school drop-out rate was 43
per cent. The school system as a whole was in a mess following the trauma of desegregation in the 1970s, which led to
violence as black pupils were bused into schools across the
city. There was pressure on the one hand from local people
to share in the new wealth that was being brought into
Boston plus 'white flight' of middle-class residents from inner-
city neighbourhoods, while on the other hand there were
developing labour shortages. Prompted by the Private Industry Council, the education authorities therefore started the
Compact in 1982 whereby schools made formal agreements
with employers to improve the grades and attendance of their
pupils in return for guaranteed jobs. As it turns out, the
schools have found it hard to deliver their side of the bargain,
while employers have had to fill the jobs they needed anyway,
though Compact may have improved the matching of jobs to
school-leavers.

In London, where a similar Dockland redevelopment was
under way, the Inner London Education Authority thought
Compact would be an effective means to commit incoming
firms to employing local youngsters. In addition, the London
Education Business Partnership between the authority and
several London companies was set up as an alternative to
the government's proposals for City Technology Colleges in
the capital. Six schools and one further education college
were joined together in a pioneering consortium with LEBP
firms to found the East London Compact in 1987. This model
was reluctantly acknowledged by the government when it

announced the extension of Compact nationwide the following year at an annual cost of £3 million. The government's reluctance stemmed from an unwillingness to acknowledge any positive contribution by the ILEA, which it was determined to abolish in the face of a popular but ultimately unsuccessful parental campaign to save it.

For their side of the Compact, or bargain, fourth- and fifth-year pupils must undertake to complete all their coursework, including a community project as part of a personal, social and health education course, two weeks' work experience, and to meet all their homework deadlines to achieve graded results in their examinations. They are also required to aim for 85 per cent attendance and 90 per cent punctuality in their last two years, all of which is detailed in a record of achievement. Thus the formally stated aims of the Compact are what the participating schools would already be trying to achieve for their pupils.

For their part, while they do not explicitly guarantee employment, employers undertake to give priority in job offers to those school-leavers who achieve the educational targets. This can mean a guaranteed interview or a reserved place on a company-run Youth Training scheme. Participating employers also support school–industry links with the schools involved, by offering work experience, work shadowing, holiday jobs and teacher–industry exchanges. They also promise equal opportunities in recruitment, consideration to school-leavers with special educational needs, and they undertake to provide permanent jobs with further education and training opportunities. These last are also no more than they should be doing, although the Compact may have the advantage of drawing attention to their commitment to these goals.

Compacts need to persuade young people, as well as their parents and teachers, that they will get more out of school than if the Compact did not exist. Some Compacts are therefore looking at 'value added' YT, such as offering inner-city school-leavers employed-status schemes to which they would not otherwise have had access. Several companies involved are enthusiastic about 'flexing-up' YT to meet their particular requirements and as a result they plan to offer part-time and three-year YT. But this loosening-up of YT, already seen to be taking place through the locally based Training and Enterprise Councils, which may also take over the running of Compacts, is also contributing to the demise of the scheme as a coherent and standard national programme.

Results from Compacts so far purport to be positive, although ILEA's own detailed analysis recorded that contracted employment with an original sponsoring employer was rare. This is not necessarily the main point, however. An early HMI assessment found that the scheme had a significant impact on those schools taking part. Involvement in Compacts had contributed to developments in personal, social and health education, careers work, community service and the monitoring of exam course work and homework as detailed in the record of achievement. Improvements in attendance, punctuality and staying-on rates (though this is not one of the Compact's formal intentions) were also claimed. In addition, the HMI report noted that Compacts had the virtue of being cheap to set up and run. They did however record that 'senior staff at schools need to secure more commitment from teachers to Compacts if they are to meet their full potential'.

Teachers' reactions have indeed been mixed. At one extreme Compacts have been denounced as *The Gateway to Slave Labour*. This radical left publication saw them as putting teachers in the position of gatekeepers to pupils' future employment prospects. However, while Compacts formalise the relationship between school attendance and punctuality that can be important in gaining access to work, they do not enforce a legally binding contract upon either of their participants. Regular school attendance and exam qualifications have always had an effect on subsequent employment, as shown by countless studies revealing the association of truancy and lack of qualifications with subsequent youth unemployment.

'The trouble with the Compact', said a teacher at one of

the East London schools involved, 'is that the kids it could help are either so disillusioned we don't see them any more, or else they've got themselves fixed up with jobs for when they leave anyway. The ones already attending and working well aren't particularly interested in it because they don't want to leave but aim to go on to college. So there has been no fundamental change in attitude or attendance. We used to have work experience plus firms and training schemes visiting the school before too. I'm not so sure about insurance salesmen type of people coming in to advertise their YTS. Admittedly this is what a lot of the kids are heading for but I don't like this rush to get them signed up.'

Other teachers, while labouring under no illusions about the scheme, considered it had benefited their schools. 'Of course, most of the companies are in it for the publicity. Once Prince Charles became involved, lots of firms wanted to get in on the act. But we have managed to get things out of them. Our department got a new computer and they have arranged some great visits and speakers for the pupils. It's given the kids a lot of confidence. I think too the business people have learnt a lot. They didn't know anything about schools like this. They can't believe it when they see what things are like – sharing one set of books among six classes, for instance.'

Said a careers teacher in one school, 'Compact is our chance to crack the City of London jobs market'. Or, as a teacher union representative put it, 'Compact may help to overcome a certain preference of City firms for recruiting from the leafy suburbs'.

Similarly, teachers record mixed feelings about their own work experience which they too undertook as part of Compact. 'I went to a hotel to find out about the workings of the hotel industry and I ended up shelling peas for two weeks', recalled one long-suffering religious education teacher. While he was undergoing this penance, the head of home economics in the same school made 60 gallons of custard while her classes were being covered by a supply teacher. This is not what work experience for teachers is supposed to be about.

'Like pupils, teachers must be matched to their placement', commented the careers teacher. 'It helps if you're interested in the placement', agreed a science teacher he had placed. 'I mean, I can now cook a mean steak Diane – that's why I went to the hotel kitchens, to acquire some *cordon bleu* cookery from an expert. But it will benefit my pupils as well because they're following a modular science course which includes food science and I'm planning a return visit by the head chef to the school.' It has been suggested that work experience undertaken by teachers has contributed to the mounting losses from the profession, as teachers on work experience have discovered opportunities and offers of employment outside the classroom.

Apart from the fall in teachers' earnings in relation to other occupations, another factor encouraging such losses to the profession is the purported low morale of the teaching force. Teachers have been routinely denigrated by governments ever since they were blamed during the 1970s for the unemployment figures of former pupils, which has contributed to a loss of respect and public confidence in teachers and education generally. In part, the scapegoating of schools for failing to provide solutions to society's problems, ranging from unemployment to football hooliganism, followed the equally unrealistic expectation, encouraged during the educational expansion of the 1960s, that schools could solve all of these problems for society. One consequence of this slide in their professional status has been the loss of what has been called the 'teacher paradigm', whereby most pupils respected a teacher's authority as being fair exchange for the knowledge necessary to pass examinations guaranteeing entry to desirable and secure occupations. The minority of pupils who did not accept the terms of this informal contract anticipated a future of unskilled, 'dead end' jobs. In most comprehensive schools they could be jollied along into compliance with school norms by attending a combination of special classes in more practical subjects, work experience and so-called 'sin bins'.

When the youth labour market collapsed in the 1970s the

carrot of 'study-hard-for-a-good-job-when-you-leave-school' could no longer be held out to all pupils by teachers. This collapse precipitated a crisis in the state secondary schools to which the vocational phase of education policy was an answer. Now that the economy has revived, in some areas at least, it has done so on a different basis from the previous demand from industry for school-leavers who could be sorted by the schools 20:40:40. This ratio corresponded to the traditional hierarchy in manufacturing industry between non-manual, skilled manual and unskilled manual labour.

Compacts and other developments in vocational education being reviewed here can be seen as part of an effort by schools and society to find new relations to a new pattern of employment. In this new pattern the demand for a top 20 per cent certified by way of higher education for administrative and professional non-manual employment may have remained constant, but the traditional demand for skilled manual employment for boys has much reduced, while its equivalent for girls of a good office job has expanded. Unskilled manual work is also less in demand. There is currently in existence a large semi-skilled job market requiring the flexible and adaptable workers who have been seen to be so sought after by employers.

However, like so many of the links between schools and industry introduced during the vocational phase of 1976–87, Compact is undermined by the latest education reforms which posit parents rather than employers as the 'consumers' of education. The market they seek to reinforce is not the labour market, which can perhaps now be left to look after itself since there is no longer such a threatening surplus of unemployed youth, but the education market, in which it is intended schools should now compete with one another for survival by attracting a reduced number of pupils. The average test scores which will be aggregated and published for each school will, it is planned, give parents a yardstick by which to judge school performance. Unconstrained choice between schools will allow parents to withdraw their children from the lowest-scoring schools and send them to the more successful, thus causing overall standards to rise and forcing the bad schools to close.

Rather than this optimistic scenario drawn by the supporters of current education reform, a growing divergence is predicted by its opponents, between two types of state school in the education market: the successful, opted-out, reborn grammar schools on the one hand and the struggling, under-funded, council schools on the other. The former will prepare their pupils for entry via higher education to careers in a secure, professional and administrative core of employment, while the latter will provide flexible and intermittent labour via YT for a semi-skilled periphery.

But even if this bleak scenario is avoided and the rosiest dreams of the educational reformers are realised, the 'standards' set by the new education consumers' market for parents would not be the same as the demands which employers as consumers make of the schools. Vague and general though these are, they do not include proficiency in an outdated and academic curriculum. This may succeed in raising academic standards, but it has little to do with the latest needs of industry or the demands which the rapidly accelerating development of society and technology places upon its future citizens.

Work experience

Work experience forms an important part of Compact as well as a component of TVEI and pre-vocational courses in schools and colleges such as the CPVE. Some 300,000 pupils already undertake work experience for at least two weeks every year and it is the intention of the enterprising Department of Trade and Industry to double that number. The DTI also wants 10 per cent of all teachers to engage in two weeks' work experience annually, although how this is ever to be achieved remains unclear.

The whole *raison d'être* of work experience is in fact rather obscure. Kenneth Baker, the former Minister of Education, considered that 'Teachers find work experience immensely valuable because many of them go straight from schools to

college and so know nothing about industry'. Mr Baker's previous enthusiasm for the benefits of work experience was
tempered however by his advocacy of the new National Curriculum. 'I have to say', he told a conference in May 1988,
'that I doubt many schools will be able to devote much time
to workplace activities unless they contribute explicitly to
curriculum objectives.'

As part of the rethinking of work experience in the light
of new circumstances, the School Curriculum Industry Partnership undertook a review of work experience, as a result of
which they pinpointed a variety of aims for work experience
advocated by the many organisations that run and support
it.

In some schools, work experience is linked to coherent programmes of study in which it aims to deepen understanding
of scientific and technical processes or of social organisation
at work by means of practical participation and observation.
The most effective examples were found in English, mathematics and social studies, where work experience was used
to conduct research into topics being covered within the classroom. Surprisingly, the survey revealed that this was not
often achieved within TVEI, where it might be expected that
this kind of integration would be more common than
elsewhere.

Other schools aimed to enhance pupil motivation by showing them through work experience the relevance and practical application of subjects which they were learning in the
detached and theoretical environment of the classroom or
laboratory. Here, as one prospectus stated, 'work experience
is seen as an opportunity for pupils to relate prior learning
to real world applications and begin to understand the need
to take care of their own learning, that is to learn how to
learn'. This was related to schools where the aim of work
experience was formulated as aiding the maturation of pupils'
personal and social development. One teachers' union recognised that working alongside adults other than teachers can
'contribute powerfully to young people's social development'.

As far as more specifically vocational intentions are concerned, in many schools work experience is linked to programmes of careers education, where work experience can help pupils in their career choice. It can either confirm the occupation to which they aspire or, alternatively, show them that what they had thought they wanted to do was not as they had imagined it.

The Trades Union Congress supports work experience, even though it tends to encourage children to work for no pay. Pupils can, says a TUC document, 'find out how different work places are organised, what the work processes are, what social relations at work are like, and what part trade unions play at the workplace'. This is also seen in local terms by HMI as 'promoting a knowledge of the industrial, commercial and public employers in the area and understanding how they function'.

Experience of work can broaden the range of occupations which pupils are prepared to consider. This is particularly relevant when challenging the traditional sex-stereotyping of occupations: 'An important opportunity for girls to gain experience in work traditionally reserved for men and for boys to be placed in traditionally female areas of employment', as the TUC says. This is similar to the related aim of allowing pupils to sample a range of occupations. Since only two weeks per year of work experience out of school is currently permitted by law for 14–16-year-olds, there is usually not time for this during term, except perhaps by means of short visits. Thus many schools commonly orient placements towards pupils' preferred vocational interests where that is possible. The TUC does not favour this practice, nor does it lend support to work experience being used for students to acquire skills and knowledge related to a particular occupational area.

Similarly, the Department of Education and Science states in its guidelines that, 'work experience must not be seen as a preparation for any particular job or career ... [Nor] as a means of entry to any particular job or career.' In fact, such a use of work experience is only common on specifically vocational courses in colleges and training schemes. The wider aim of preparing school-leavers to make the transition to work is more generally endorsed.

It is instructive to compare these officially stated aims for work experience with actual experiences of pupils in London on a 'bridging course' between school, college and work. While they were particularly positive in their estimation of the work experience that formed a component part of the course, their reasons for that evaluation were not necessarily those that would be expected.

'I had a lovely time in the old people's day centre. It showed you how much you have to care about old people. I liked being with mentally handicapped kids too, but I didn't like infants' school so much.'

'Work experience was pretty good in a print firm and then double-glazing. It didn't give me an idea of what I wanted to do but it gave me an idea of what you've got coming when you're left at work for the rest of your life. When you're at school everything's done for you and you don't think about anything. Your old girl buys everything for you, but when you leave you've got to knock your bollocks off for it. It showed you what the governors were like as well – ponces. They try to take advantage of you on work experience. Because they're not paying you they try to get you to do their work for nothing.'

Most commonly, 'It was less boring than school and it got you away from school for a while just doing something that you wanted to do'.

At the time that these views were recorded, unemployment was high locally and thus several pupils had regarded their work experience as a means to get a job. In some cases it had helped them to do so, while in others, part-time evening and Saturday work had already given them the experience required for a successful application. Others were disappointed not to find work in the firm to which they were sent from school: 'I keep 'phoning the bloke but there's nothing going.' 'I went back to the office but someone had taken my place.' 'They said I could work in the nursery if I wanted to but I didn't fancy it voluntarily.'

School-leavers were contacted later to find out what use their work experience had been to them. In retrospect,

'It wasn't like real work, not work work. You used to laze about much more. It was good but no use.'

'I thought it would help me, having done my work experience in a travel agent but when I applied for a job they only asked me what exams I'd got. I showed them my reference from work experience but they didn't take any notice.'

'When I went to work in an office they did everything different to the way they did at the office I went to on work experience. The whole system was different with different machines and everything.'

'Work experience might've been alright if I'd've gone in for printing. I could've said I've had that experience, but I've forgotten it all now. It would've been alright if I'd got a job out of it. As it was, it was just a waste of time.'

This more sceptical verdict was typical. Often, 'You don't need experience to work where I am now'.

In many schools work experience has become something that everyone does at some stage in their school career. Usually this is at the end of the fourth year, when exams are over and all the other local schools are competing to find worthwhile placements for their pupils.

'It is unusual to find a school where systematic arrangements have been made in the curriculum to help students relate what has often been an important learning experience to wider contexts which would aid them in interpreting what happened to them', states a 1989 study by Leeds University. It concludes: 'Although work experience has made considerable demands on school resources, it has had limited influence upon the curriculum'.

It has also not escaped the notice of researchers that 'While a few years ago school-leavers without qualifications of any kind had no difficulty in getting jobs, many of them are now deemed to need "work experience" before they can be regarded as employable'. With the demographic drop in the supply of youth labour, this is now less likely to be the case in regions where there is some buoyancy in the economy.

Since work experience is undertaken voluntarily, placements have to suit individual pupils' own preferences as far as possible, unless they can be persuaded to do something in which they have not expressed an interest. Places are therefore often selected by students' ability, the more academic ones going into office and technical posts while the less academic do more practical work. This only serves further to confirm the social divisions that even the most comprehensive schools cannot help reinforcing through the examination system and by their selection for further study.

Many parents who hope that their children will do well in examinations see no point in them breaking off their studies for two weeks, or for a day a week over a term, to do something they regard as an irrelevance. In the sixth form work experience is usually restricted to the one-year pre-vocational courses, like CPVE, and does not fit into the intensive study required for A levels.

With the difficulties in finding placements where unemployment is high and in competition with other schools and colleges, some institutions resort to simulated work experience. In one extraordinary example, a college in Coventry set up its own 'lightbox assembly' in a converted lecture room: 'Here trainees construct, wire and test equipment, then package it and write the accompanying advice notes. The organisation is tight and efficient, and a convincing assembly regime is produced. When the lightboxes reach their destination in the main College building they are dismantled and their components fed back for assembly', commended the Further Education Unit's *Suggestions for Organisers of Schemes of UVP*.

Rather than this modern version of digging holes and filling them in again, simulations more commonly take the form of mini-enterprises. At Solihull's Kingshurst CTC, for instance, the whole first year abandoned their normal timetable for a week 'to research, produce and market' yoghurt. Teams of children were formed and given targets: for example, the advertising and marketing team was briefed 'to produce sufficient product to allow a full-scale market research test'.

Mini-enterprise is held by its advocates to release enormous amounts of student energy and imagination in pursuit of the few pounds the participant shareholders in the enterprise can manage to raise by a week's work. The idea for mini-enterprise came from the USA and was introduced to schools in this country in the 1960s. It received a boost recently from the government's support for 'enterprise culture': one aim of Industry Year in 1986, for example, was to see every secondary school running at least one mini-company. As a result more than 20,000 children annually now form themselves into 800 companies, an activity supported by its own charity, Young Enterprise. The Midland Bank has recently produced a kit containing manuals, forms, share certificates, etc., for YE participants, while other banks, such as Lloyds, are willing to operate company accounts free of charge and even offer small loans as incentives.

'Achievers', as YE participants are called, learn how to form a company, setting up a Memorandum and Articles of Association. They elect their own officers, prepare a budget, buy materials, and hire premises and the necessary equipment (usually at nominal rates). At the end of the operation the company is properly wound up with the presentation of final accounts, balance sheet, report to the directors and declaration of a dividend to the shareholders. It does not matter so much what is actually produced, but most groups concentrate on handicrafts such as woodwork, pottery or macrame, or they print T-shirts or badges; fish tanks and herbaria are also popular. Such activities are a means to accumulate transferable skills on TVEI and CPVE profiles. They also contribute towards what one journalist commentator called 'that now familiar litany of skills – in communication, problem-solving, decision-making, team work and accountability – which are considered indispensable for the creation of an "enterprise economy" '.

HMI's 1990 report on mini-enterprises was 'highly critical'

of the way these are set up in both primary and secondary schools. 'There is a danger', they wrote, 'of cluttering primary classrooms with a multitude of adult concerns. In particular, the use of profit as the sole criterion to judge success or failure of an enterprise is inappropriate.' While in secondary schools they considered mini-enterprise was 'not giving a realistic picture of the realities of the market place'.

Work experience may also be obtained by pupils in the more altruistic area of community service such as work in day nurseries, old people's homes and conservation schemes. Although these may be regarded as community service projects rather than work experience, they achieve the same ends as far as participants are concerned. There are also the same problems of finding something to which to make a real contribution in a short time without disrupting study timetables. Often it is the pupils of whom little is expected elsewhere who reveal unexpected funds of selfless support for others on such community work placements. The occupations to which they could actually lead, however, are unfortunately invariably of low status and badly paid.

Much work experience originated and expanded because of a belief that there was a problem of 'transition' between school and work, and this was seen as a 'cultural gap' which pupils needed help to bridge. Induction by work experience could facilitate the transition between school and work that was discussed at such length. In fact, in many cases if there was a problem of transition it was that of making a more than physical transition into school and its norms and values. If pupil aspirations and expectations lagged behind a changing industrial landscape, schools, which are naturally conservative institutions concerned with the communication of past culture to the future generations, often lagged yet further behind.

It often continues to be the case that, as Michael Carter wrote in his classic account of the education and employment of young people in the 1960s, *Home, School and Work*, 'For most young people there is a basic continuity in their experience at home, at school and at work'. He was describing a traditional industrial community in Sheffield, where many sons followed their fathers into the factories. But it is still true that 'Their particular occupations were not a vital matter for a large number of children . . . What was important was the status which being a worker conferred.'

After the recession and collapse of many traditional employments, with whole regions where any job is better than no job, and with the flexibility and adaptability that is expected of a growing peripheral workforce, this is possibly even more true today. This poses a particular problem for careers education.

Careers education and the Careers Service

The position of careers education within schools and their relation to the Careers Service acts as a barometer indicating the importance attached to vocational education at different times. The Careers Service is a national service administered locally. It began life as the Juvenile Employment Bureau, a specialised section of the Labour Exchanges set up before the First World War, and was renamed the Youth Employment Service after the Second World War. The change of name to Careers Service in 1974 reflected the growing importance of vocational guidance to its 3,500 careers officers. The emphasis upon equal opportunities through comprehensive education meant that careers, and not just employment, should be made available to all school-leavers.

At the same time the Service has forged closer links with the schools by coming under the control of the local education authorities. The LEAs finance its work in schools, even though it is still under the direction and inspection of the Department of Employment. The Careers Service has also branched out to embrace further education and the polytechnics and other higher education colleges which then came under the control of the local authorities.

The bread and butter of Careers Service work remained in the schools, with officers interviewing pupils in their last years and enabling the Service to integrate its efforts more closely with growing careers departments and courses. In

Coventry this process went so far as to base all careers officers in the schools. The Inner London Education Authority also experimented with these 'School to Work Liaison Officers', as it called them.

However, as unemployment rose during the 1970s there were suggestions that the Service should be abolished, thereby saving annual costs equivalent to the Civil List (approximately £80 million). Abolition would have heralded the abandonment of any pretence that careers were available any longer to young people. Instead of this drastic denouement, extra money was put into the service by the Department of Employment for outreach by detached employment officers and other work with the unemployed. Careers officers also assumed a new role as the major referral point for young people into YTS which gave them further importance in schools, until the introduction of an academic National Curriculum relegated careers education to the limbo of a cross-curricular theme.

The swing away from vocational education towards a more academic curriculum precludes the question of the relation of schools to the economy, which had at least begun to be addressed during the vocational period of educational policy. In the past, tripartite system of schooling, allocation to particular types of school, or to streams within schools, gave pupils clear signals of the vocational aspirations which were considered appropriate for them. This may also be the effect of the 'differentiation' between schools which the educational reforms are intended to encourage.

Career choices for young people are limited in the regions where traditional industries have declined and employers prefer women and other older part-timers for many jobs in the new service industries. This makes it difficult for careers officers to sustain their belief in the individual developmental processes of vocational choice. Yet this is their official ideology as expressed, for instance, by the Schools Council in one of its last publications in 1985 which stated, 'Careers education is about enabling individual growth and development'. Careers officers strongly resist going back to a role of match-

63

ing suitable individuals with available jobs. As one practitioner emphasised: 'Ensuring that future manpower requirements are satisfied is not the careers counsellor's job. His responsibility is to his students. These two roles, the counsellor and the recruiter, are quite distinct and their goals are incompatible.' Some of those involved have gone so far as to argue for the complete opposite to serving the needs of industry, wanting instead to change the existing structures of employment for the benefit of the employees.

At the opposite pole to this approach stands that of manpower planning. Rather than the aspirations of individuals, manpower planners seek to serve the perceived needs of employers. The vocational preferences of individuals are, to the manpower planner, so many brakes upon achieving a fully flexible labour force.

In a free market, however, manpower planning proper can only take place in the state sector. For example, by taking a policy decision in 1981 to cut back on secondary teacher-training by reducing courses to only one year, the government substantially contributed to teacher shortages by mid-decade.

Yet manpower planners can highlight the general needs of the economy; for example the need for more flexible labour, or for women to enter occupations that were previously closed to them but where there are now labour shortages. Under the reign of the Manpower Services Commission, which tried for the first time to implement a policy of comprehensive manpower planning, it was the accepted wisdom that, to be effective, intervention needed to occur as early as possible in the schools.

Notwithstanding their fundamental conflict of approach, careers counsellors and manpower planners could agree that instead of aiding clients to make their own definite vocational choice, they could be supported into adopting a flexible and open-minded attitude. They could be helped to face the prospect of perpetual change of employment throughout their working lives. This will require repeated training and retraining to keep up with the latest changes in technology. Occupational counselling would then have a lifelong role, rather than be restricted to helping to crystallise young people's initial choice; thus, instead of a single, once and forever event, vocational choice becomes a continuous process.

As it stands, the Service has a statutory duty only to work with those under 18 and to inform them and their parents about jobs, training and further and higher education courses. After age 18, local authorities are permitted but not mandated by the 1974 Employment and Training Act to provide further vocational guidance. There is no publicly funded vocational guidance service for adults: most Occupational Guidance Units for adults were wound up in the early 1980s, though they still function in some big city Jobcentres. Private services also exist, but they can be expensive.

For students in their later years at school or college the Careers Service has three main roles. Careers officers give guidance and information to those who have not made up their minds about what they want to do when they leave school. For those who have made that decision, they provide information on the best way of realising their choice. Lastly, they attempt to place their clients in the jobs of their choice.

The careers office attempts to keep in touch with clients throughout their early working lives. There are specialist officers working with the unemployed, sixth-formers and in further and special education. Job vacancies suitable for young people are normally notified to the careers office rather than to Jobcentres. In an unequal and segmented labour market, the Service attempts to promote equal opportunities for all young people irrespective of race, sex or disability.

For employers, the local careers office provides a free service, pre-screening recruits for the vacancies on offer and which are suitable for young people. The office advises them on the timing and planning of recruitment, recommends suitable wage rates for young workers and disseminates information about the latest changes in education and training, including the subsidies, allowances and special programmes that may be available, as well as on such employment legislation as remains to protect the interests of young workers. Visits to employers' premises and regular contact with them help local careers offices to build up a bank of local labour market information which has become increasingly computerised and thus more widely available to the youth service and schools.

In schools and colleges careers officers conduct over a million careers interviews annually with students. Their first contact is usually in the third year at school when pupils make their option choices for examination subjects. With all pupils supposed to be continuing with the subjects on the National Curriculum there will be less room for choice, and the role of careers officers and careers teachers may as a result be substantially reduced.

Full careers interviews are held in the fourth and fifth years, at which aptitude tests, interest and personality inventories are used to assist the interviewer in assessing pupils' potential. These may also be administered to whole classes as part of a programme of careers teaching. The officer usually visits the school several times and sees a pupil at least twice. If they stay on into the sixth form, students are normally interviewed again. Yet because they do not have to make a definite career choice until two, five, six or seven years later, sixth formers and under- and post-graduates characteristically remain open-minded about their job aims. This is encouraged by the ideal of education for its own sake, which often masks what is actually an apprenticeship in professional occupational norms. There remains a conflict in schools between teachers and the careers office for the more academic pupils who can most easily be placed in employment, but whom the school wishes to retain to add to its prestigious tally of entrants to higher education.

For teachers and lecturers, careers officers provide training and advice. They help to devise careers education programmes and keep the schools up to date with developments in local employment and training opportunities and they offer practical help in programmes of education involving visits to and from workplaces and to find work experience placements. Like careers teachers, they support job applicants, not only through the ubiquitous practice-in-writing-a-letter-of-application but also more imaginative exercises, like videoing trial interviews and role play. The Careers Service is also the main channel of occupational information between employers and schools, thus enabling the compilation of careers libraries in most secondary schools which are supplemented by films, videos and computer information.

Despite all this effort, vocational expectations rarely match outcomes, except in traditional and closed communities like mining, fishing or agricultural villages, or among the British ruling class. Perhaps this is because ideas remain fixed in the past, while reality changes in unforeseen directions. Another reason for the low congruence of expectations with outcomes is the pyramid structure of opportunities, which means that the majority of those who aim high are bound to be disappointed. Even in Sheffield in the 1960s, only 80 of the 200 school leavers followed up by Carter were in the occupation they had stated as their preference in interview with the youth employment officer. Now, as then, more girls than boys end up in occupations of their choice, largely because their aspirations for work are characteristically lower. In a nationwide child development sample of 17,000 children born in one week of March 1958, only 32 per cent overall were found to be in work for which they had expressed a preference in their last year at school seven years earlier.

Of course, aspirations change throughout life, from the authority models of infant school pupils (typically – teacher, policeman) through fantasy figures in junior and lower secondary (air-hostess, footballer) to a more settled choice in a general work area for most fourth and fifth formers. These aspirations are influenced by those who are important in young people's lives, more usually parents than careers officers, however well informed they may be. However, careers officers exercise more influence than teachers on most school students – though careers teachers have more influence than other teachers. Parents' and children's views of the local labour market tend to be very well-informed, but about three years out of date. Parents continue to think in terms of what was available in their own youth, such as apprenticeship and night school, rather than in terms of present-day opportunities.

Actual job choice, if that is an appropriate term, is in the majority of cases guided more by the informal processes of word of mouth than the formal local placement services. Careers offices, by their association with Youth Training, may even become a last resort for many youngsters in some areas. There are also competing commercial employment agencies, advertising and the media which, while they do not place very many young people, since there is little money to be made out of it, do exercise an influence over their job choice.

The careers interview for every pupil in school, which is the linchpin of Careers Service work and often includes parents, 'does not', as Carter described it, 'consist of three or four rational and disinterested beings gathered together to evaluate the evidence and deliberate upon a policy. It usually consists of people from different classes, with different norms, different ways of speaking and dressing, all playing different roles.' In this situation the careers officer often has a difficult job persuading children to lower their aspirations to what is actually available. 'The enthusiast is not prepared to hear anything which detracts from his ideas of what the job will be like', while the officer tries to pin down the young person's choice to some specific vacancy.

Consequently, careers officers are often blamed for keeping youngsters back. In a recent survey of 100 black and Asian journalists working in the British media, for instance, several had been advised in careers interviews not to persist in their ambition to become journalists. In one such case, when an aspiring pupil stated a preference to work in television, he was offered a job in an electrical repairs shop!

The end result may be that, as Carter concluded, 'the job pattern depends as much, if not more, upon fortuity and aimless or uninformed drifting as upon deliberate intention and design'. However, this is not to denigrate the efforts of the Careers Service, just as marriage counsellors cannot be blamed for the high rate of divorce. Without them, things would be even worse.

In fact, in a situation of increasingly rapid economic and social transformation, the task of helping individuals prepare for and adapt to change becomes even more vital, particularly as, to ensure society's future survival, unprecedented changes in production and consumption become unavoidable. Such changes will require the most comprehensive manpower planning from above supported by popular participation from below. While they may have a role to play in helping people adjust to these changes, this can hardly be the responsibility of the Careers and employment services alone.

Vocational qualifications

Employers have been reluctant to abandon their habit of recruiting for many jobs on the basis of grades obtained in written examinations. For most of them, secondary school examinations – including the new GCSEs – are indicators of attitudes rather than abilities. They demonstrate the self-discipline and sustained application necessary to complete the course, rather than any practical competence or theoretical knowledge actually required in the occupations for which they are qualifications.

Although the General Certificate of Secondary Education was introduced in 1986 for everyone in their fifth year at school, the first question that employers asked was how did it correspond to the old division between O levels and CSEs. Thus grade C in the new exam quickly became the cut-off point for application to many jobs for which O-level passes had been required previously. Grades D to G, while they might represent a significant achievement for many entrants, quickly came to be regarded as worthless.

This problem of credibility afflicts the most ambitious attempt to introduce coherence into the maze of vocational qualifications in order to make them continuous with academic and professional qualifications through the National Council for Vocational Qualifications (NCVQ). This was set up by the Department of Employment in 1986 following a review of all existing vocational qualifications in England and Wales. It recommended bringing all such qualifications within a National Vocational Qualification framework, the first four levels of which were to be operational for most occupations by 1991. The intention is for this framework to become the main means by which the standards and scope of vocational qualifications are judged by employers and trade unions, trainees and students in training and education, as well as by local and national government.

Although supported by the Department of Employment, the NCVQ is not itself an examining or validating body, nor has it any statutory powers. It has had to work on a voluntary basis with the various competing examination boards and awarding bodies to establish an agreed system of credit accumulation, but its lack of power has hampered progress towards this aim. All the major awarding bodies, however, like the Business and Technician Education Council and the City and Guilds Institute, have co-operated to a point, with the result that their existing qualifications will receive the NCVQ's 'kitemark' (modelled on the British Standards Authority sign). This recognises them as comprising so many units of competence, while new assessments will also be certified in the same terms. By simply endorsing existing qualifications NCVQ risks its own redundancy, but it cannot afford to alienate those upon whose voluntary co-operation it depends.

Eventually it is hoped to phase in one homogeneous scheme of qualifications within which degree-level, professional qualifications will correspond to level 5. As a rule of thumb, BTEC National and Higher National Certificates and Diplomas are equivalent to technician levels 3 and 4, City and Guilds and other apprenticeship qualifications equate with craft level 2 and 'pre-vocational', general preparatory qualifications, such as the CPVE, match level 1.

Again, however, NCVQ's lack of power over the industrial lead bodies (ILBs) developing these qualifications for their various sectors means that they have moved in different directions in their requirements for competence at different levels. Hence content, scope and breadth of qualification at the same level can differ markedly in different occupational areas, which complicates the NCVQ's aim of credit-transfer between different examining and evaluating bodies.

National Vocational Qualifications and the credits towards them can all be entered in a National Record of Vocational Achievement (NROVA; supposed to be issued to all Youth Trainees). This could possibly be made continuous with school records of achievement in a vocational system which is intended to overcome the distinctions between educational institutions and training in work. NROVAs are designed to record individuals' cumulative achievements of competence throughout their working lives so as to allow for continuous training and retraining. There are no upper or lower age limits to beginning this process, nor do NVQs prescribe the time to be spent in education, training or work before an award can be made. Access is intended to be open to people of all ages, who are to be encouraged to learn at their own pace. Evidence of prior learning is accepted, so that trainees do not need to waste time repeating things they have already shown they can do. With flexible entry, training would ideally be tailor-made for individuals with different work and life experiences. There should be, say the Council's guidelines, 'no overt or covert discriminatory practices with regard to gender, race, and creed, or those with special needs, built into the specification of statements of competence or assessment procedures'. These can be undertaken in a language other than English, 'Provided that clear evidence is available that the candidate is competent in English to the standard required for performance in employment throughout the UK'.

The principle upon which these NVQs are awarded is that each represents a statement of competence of what the holder can do. The national standards of competence which are set for various levels of certification are agreed by those on both sides of industry – employers and trade unions – in the employment to which they apply. This allows those who are conversant with the occupations to which an award relates to define what the appropriate standards should be, on the reasonable assumption that they are the only group of people who really understand what is required and the levels of performance that are needed.

In practice, some of these industrial lead bodies that are supposed to represent an entire industrial or commercial sector are rather narrow, and hence open to question by other employers. It is genuinely difficult to get full representation of an occupational area, for example retailing, which covers large and small companies alike. Some of the large employers who already have their own training schemes tend to plough their own furrow, regardless of what the NCVQ thinks of them.

Allowing each industry to take the lead in its own sector has created a problem of transfer between occupations. In an effort to achieve consistency across sectors, the NCVQ is now attempting to devise 'generic units of competence' not based on specific competencies.

What the ILBs prescribe are the outcomes of learning in the standards of performance which need to be assessed. They do not decide the syllabus or programme of learning which should lead to this outcome. The task of providing learning experiences on structured programmes of instruction and practice is left to educators and trainers. This principle is nowadays couched in terms of regard for their professional expertise. But when the Department of Employment first set up the NCVQ, the aggressive emphasis upon outcomes alienated those in both further education and the training community who were expected to provide these results.

Like the programmes planned for Youth Training, NVQs are based upon a foundation of a set of core units common to most occupations in the area of competence. To these can be added various optional units relevant to a particular specialisation or occupation within the general area of competence.

Lower-level NVQs may certify YT completion in the occupational training families where the scheme survives in any coherent national form. Level 1 corresponds to the stated aims for first-year YT by providing a broad foundation in the occupational area, primarily for progression; these activities will necessarily be routine and predictable. Level 2 might correspond to the second year of YT planned for many occupations by recognising competence in a broader and more demanding range of work activities. Beyond that, level 3 covers work activities that are more complex and non-routine, including 'supervisory competence'. Level 4 extends to specialised technical and professional work, including those associated with design and planning and reaching into the lower levels of management.

In one of his last pronouncements as Employment Secretary, Norman Fowler set the ambitious goal of two-thirds of all 16-year-old school-leavers attaining level 2 NVQ by 1992 in or out of employment. By the same date a quarter of young people should also have reached level 3. By 1995 all 18-year-olds should have a recognised qualification at level 2 and half of them at level 3. Unfortunately it is unlikely these targets will be met.

Elements of competence which comprise a unit for award are listed in a statement of competence which indicates the standards required for competent performance. These statements have on the one hand to be sufficiently precise so as to allow unambiguous interpretation by different awarding bodies, assessors, trainers and trainees. On the other hand, they cannot be so detailed that they only relate to a specific task or job with a particular machine in one organisation or location, but should apply to an occupation as a whole. The difficulties of balancing these conflicting demands in a practical and credible way cannot be underestimated.

While they also have to be flexible enough to accommodate new and emerging employment requirements, the awards need to relate to awards at other levels within the same area of competence. In fact the relationship and links between awards should be made explicit so as to facilitate progression.

Assessment is practical: if the competence involves doing something, such as driving a truck or serving a customer, the assessor has to observe behaviour in the normal workplace environment. Thus assessment can only be as good as the workplace where it occurs, added to which there may not always be the opportunity to demonstrate to an assessor all the competencies which are required. As a result, several pilot projects are being set up in an attempt to resolve the uncertainties surrounding work-based learning and assessment. Conditions often have to be simulated in assessment centres: for example, the Construction Industry Training Board has established a network of well-equipped skill-testing centres to assess its apprenticeship-cum-YT.

'Accreditation is based upon evidence of achievement not learning', says the NCVQ. However, the theoretical knowledge which underpins these work activities is also supposed to be assessed. In some cases where the task could not be performed without understanding the principles of the action, theoretical knowledge can be inferred, while in others it will involve written or oral questions.

'The mode of assessment', cautions the NCVQ, 'should not place unnecessary additional demands which may inhibit or prevent a candidate from showing what they know or understand.' The Council recognises that many written tests involve literary and interpretative 'examination skills' that have nothing to do with the content of the subject being tested. Another important difference from academic qualifications is that, since all the elements of knowledge and understanding specified in the statement of competence have to be directly assessed, it will not be sufficient to sample a mere proportion of them. This, as the Council's guide to its qualifications adds, 'calls into question the practice of pass marks which is common in traditional written examinations. Assessment should ensure that a successful candidate has all the essential knowledge and understanding to be competent in employment.' This too has proved impracticable in many cases and the NCVQ is now looking again at sample testing.

Accredited NVQs to date embrace some 70 of the existing vocational qualifications in agriculture, business administration, engineering, hotel and catering, motor vehicle repair and maintenance, process, retail and textiles occupational areas. The Council is confident that this can be extended to 80 per cent of occupational areas by 1992, though whether they will actually be used in most occupations is less certain.

Employers do not necessarily welcome offers to certify the skills of their workforce. One large employer rejected the proposal for work-based accreditation on the grounds that such recognition of his employees' skills would only fuel their wage demands. While most employers are not so frank, many are unenthusiastic about undertaking work-based assessment on a large scale, except where it is seen as a means of reducing the 'off-the-job' education component of training courses.

The NCVQ's stated goal is for a system of credit accumulation to allow open access to individuals proceeding at their own pace in collecting the certification required for the practical tasks in their work. Such a flexible and modular system would allow progress both vertically towards an accumulation of practical attestation to a high level in a particular craft area, and horizontally across a range of skills. If the various credits were regarded and rewarded equally, this could form the basis for an equitable and just evaluation of skill and remuneration of labour. This is a big If, for the practical problems involved belie the NCVQ's rhetoric of opportunity.

The fact that various occupations are not accorded the same status is nowhere more apparent than in the difficulties the NCVQ has encountered in attempting to standardise vocational with professional qualifications. This task is made more necessary by the proposed standardisation of all qualifications across the European Community in 1992. The NCVQ has begun by talking to those professional bodies covering occupations with qualifications at the level of Higher National standards in the engineering, construction and financial services sector. In the latter, for instance, professional-level occupations are regulated by organisations for building societies, insurance brokers, estate agents, pensions management and accountancy. Lead bodies in these organisations can be expected, in time, to offer qualifications for accreditation by the NCVQ.

Standards of competence for a profession, as for any other occupation, must indicate what a member of that profession is capable of achieving in practice and the performance criteria necessary to assess that achievement. But professional standards are unlike specific manual tasks which can be so assessed, for example, to test whether someone can accurately type so many words per minute, or lay so many bricks in a given fashion. Professional skills are general, requiring a combination of theoretical knowledge with specific techniques in order to act within the context of a code of practice. This raises questions about why such theoretical knowledge is not considered necessary for non-professional workers who, in the ideal extension of the NVQ system, would be able to accumulate sufficient credits to transfer on to professional-level courses. It also calls into question the codes of practice which professional bodies have established and regulated and, indeed, their whole claim to professional status.

There is no generally accepted definition of what constitutes a professional body, or a profession; some occupations which make that claim – teachers for example – have no basis for it in reality. As salaried staff, without control over entry to their employment and with no independent body monitoring the standards of their members, teachers cannot yet make the same claim to professional status as, for instance, the Law Society or the BMA establishes for lawyers and doctors.

The division between professionals and other workers in fact involves a division of labour and control between those who enjoy a degree of administrative autonomy in their working conditions and those whose decisions are limited to carrying out the instructions of others. These divisions are not fixed, and are open to competition from new groups seeking to establish professional conditions for themselves. Other 'professional' groups of workers may be forced by changing conditions in their employment, or by deliberate management strategy, into the position of routine workers carrying out predefined tasks, and again teachers are a case in point. For these reasons, 'sensitivity', as the NCVQ puts it, 'remains in some professions over the extension to them of the NVQ framework'.

The NCVQ shares a more immediate problem with the rest of vocational education and training in that it no longer operates in a favourable policy environment. The National Curriculum sits uneasily alongside the NCVQ framework and its imposition upon the schools marks a reassertion of central control by the Department of Education and Science. This has ousted the Department's long-time rival the Department of Employment from the schools and colleges, and as a result will downgrade the importance of the NCVQ within education. Nevertheless, the Council is discussing with the Secondary Examination Council the linking of academic and vocational qualifications; but the TVEI, which could have built bridges between the two bodies, has been minimised in the new curriculum.

The reform of O levels to GCSEs was a step towards more practical assessment. The GCSE, insofar as it specifies learning outcomes in terms of knowledge, understanding and 'process' skills, enables educational achievement to be related to vocational competence as specified by NVQs. It would be a long stretch, but the 'benchmark' tests at 7, 11, 14 and 16 years could also, potentially, be linked to NVQs.

A danger in this widespread move towards practical assessment is that tested tasks may become so narrowly defined as to rule out all other educational considerations. The Task Group on Assessment and Testing avoided this in its recommendations for the school tests, but pressure of time and lack of resources may drive teachers towards simplifying them along the lines of the American model. Similarly, although the NCVQ says it wants to avoid a narrow conception of vocational competence, the bureaucratic weight given to the performance tasks may lead to a crude checklisting of items achieved. This would render work-based learning and assessment little more than a narrow form of work training.

Meanwhile, academic qualifications will still be given priority in selection for employment, especially the unreconstituted A levels, reform of which was rejected by the government. Thus, if and when the NCVQ succeeds in setting up a national system of vocational qualifications, NVQs will continue to be regarded as inferior to the old academic exams, even though NVQs provide more precise information of the kind which employers say they require. Unless the NCVQ can bridge the academic/vocational divide and gain the agreement of the professions and higher education to participate in the NVQ framework, it will become a (perhaps unwilling) partner in confirming the division between the academic and the vocational.

Following the simple law of supply and demand, it is possible to see the abandonment of vocational education as a reflection of the demographic drop in the number of young people. With fewer school-leavers to choose from, employers may no longer worry about appropriate qualifications for the job, certainly in the case of much of the de-skilled, peripheral workforce created by the way new technology is often applied. It will not be the case for those occupations which new technology has made more complex and demanding, even if these are a minority; nor will it allow workers to use new technology to its fullest advantage both for themselves and for the efficiency and ease of production. It will thus not raise the skill-base of the work-force as a whole.

In fact, the worst of all possible worlds could result from the education reforms. These may allow academically elite schools to compete for entrants to higher education and subsequent management roles, but beneath them the non-opted-out, 'council' schools may give up the effort to compete and will merely prepare their pupils for entry to compulsory YT and a future of low-level, semi-skilled working in insecure, peripheral and increasingly similar employments. This is a recipe not only for an inefficient and uncompetitive economy but also for an increasingly divided society.

Pre-vocational education

The terms vocational and pre-vocational education are often used loosely and interchangeably. Yet vocational education obviously has a more specific meaning of training for a particular employment, while pre-vocational has the wider sense of education for a range of occupations. There are however two distinct areas of pre-vocational education. The lower and most general level applies to all possible occupations in the economy and indeed to effective participation in society itself. The higher level of pre-vocational education prepares a selected minority for a relatively privileged and more autonomous, technical or administrative, non-manual role through the preparation for such employment given by higher education.

Before the rise of modern mass-schooling, all education, such as it was, was vocational, so that even the mysteries of the written word were reserved for a specialist caste. In Europe (and in India) priests learned an ancient language which nobody else knew because that was, literally, their vocation. No-one else needed to be literate because the priests were, and for a long time even most medieval kings were illiterate because they did not need to read in order to rule. As for the majority of the labouring population, they learnt their practical crafts by imitation within the family, where trades were passed from father to son and mother to daughter.

The division of labour was simple in terms of the numbers of different occupations as compared with today, yet it was complicated by these few roles being mutually exclusive and at the same time interdependent. By lifetimes of concentration upon one particular trade, handicrafts were developed to levels which modern society can still not surpass, even with all the technical aids at its disposal.

In industrial society a greater division of labour emerged in terms of the numbers of different occupations. These too have become increasingly subdivided to the extent that, for example, a person who repairs photocopying machines can specialise and become expert in mending a machine of one particular make, or even just fixing one particular type of fault in the machine. But despite this specialisation, it is not difficult to retrain so as to be able to repair other types of machine and other faults, especially as the standardised design of photocopiers makes fault-finding increasingly simple and replaceable parts render one machine more like another. The same microchips also make photocopiers more like washing-machines and the same chips go into a washing-machine as into a car or television.

Thus modern societies, while they may be the most highly specialised ever in terms of the range of different things which people do, are also less specialised in terms of the depth to which most people perform these tasks. There is of course still a minority of specialists, whose expertise in a very limited area depends upon prolonged practice and who are not easily replaced by anyone not sharing their particular talent. They may have developed their specialism from an early age, for example musicians and athletes. Such specialisation is no longer necessary for most occupations however, where flexibility is increasingly the rule. The interchangeability of labour in modern society rests upon a foundation of generic abilities shared by all its citizens and as a result virtually anyone can be trained and then retrained for most occupations. So even if industrial society is the most diversely specialised society that has ever existed, its variety of different occupations is prepared for by an education system that is the least specialised and the most standardised ever.

The pre-vocational skills with which mass schooling during the industrial era equipped the future workforce were those required in most jobs: functional numeracy and literacy, as well as the habits of punctuality and regularity needed for effective participation in society and employment. Beyond these basic common skills, technology has now developed to the extent that many occupations require at least keyboard familiarity with computers. It has also been predicted that foreign languages may soon be demanded for a wide range of employment. In addition, as society becomes more complex and traditional communities decay, knowledge and skills which were previously acquired informally will be incorporated into the formal school curriculum. Thus there are already courses on personal relationships, preparation for parenthood, education on drugs, the law and consumer affairs, including banking and looking after finances to prevent debt-counselling in later life. The list is endless. Careers education for all pupils in their last years could be added to it just as, at the other end of the schools system, road safety training has for long been an accepted part of primary school activities. These extra demands upon all entrants to society and the workforce lie behind the stress placed recently upon 'pre-vocational' education. The term is in fact redundant since, as has been argued, most modern mass education is pre-vocational.

Information technology has been added to the National Curriculum since it is necessary in so many occupations. As a cross-curricular theme it is supposed to interpenetrate and apply to all the subjects now considered essential for effective participation in employment and society. Obviously this is expensive and it has been argued that in order to save money there should be an attempt to concentrate IT in specialised City Technology Colleges. Rather than being pre-vocational, these would then provide vocational education with a specialised training. On Youth Training IT is similarly supposed to form a part of the foundation applicable to all occupations. Yet there is the same tendency to concentrate specialised training into the few Information Technology Centres (see pages 42–3).

'Social and life skills' are also part of the YT core. SLS, as it is called, makes explicit the pre-vocational base of knowledge and techniques that the schools have always instilled. 'Life skills' were defined by a Manpower Services Commission *Instructional Guide* as 'all those abilities, bits of information, know-how and decision making which we need to get by in life. Most of us take these basic day-to-day skills for granted but many people lack them.' This basic lack of skills was cited as the reason for trainees' failure in both education and subsequent employment. The assumption was that the deficiency of these pre-vocational skills could be remedied by youth training. Together with the general skills required in all work – literacy, numeracy, keyboard familiarity – SLS forms the pre-vocational knowledge needed before any foundation training is given in a particular occupational area. Other generic skills required for many jobs might be added, like the willingness to take responsibility and exercise supervision (though this is not usually required of young entrants, if at all) and to plan ahead and work with others.

The problem was how to assess such nebulous and general abilities if they had not already been acquired at school, for there was often no longer the opportunity to learn them informally at work in the contexts in which they would previously have been acquired as a matter of course, 'sitting by Nellie' as it was called. One solution was to break down social interactions into the subroutines involved; hence the mania for flow charts promiscuously applied to any and every situation. The problem with analysing skills into their component parts for assessment is to know where to stop, and the simplest possible term to which any decision-making process can be reduced is the binary on/off of the computer programme. While this is appropriate to the pedantic instructions which are necessary for a computer or other automated machine process to follow, it can hardly be used as the model for complex human behaviour.

Yet this model of profiling previously undefined abilities and attitudes has been widely influential beyond the 'life skills' arena. Profiling pre-vocational aptitudes, as opposed to demonstrating the competence to complete a practical task as in NVQ units, typically constitutes a key feature of TVEI provision. It is also possible that the national tests at 7, 11, 14 and 16 may be marked in just such a reductionist, checklisting manner, following the American model of computer-marked tests. Teachers themselves may even be assessed in the same way: profiles are commonly used for staff appraisal by Marks and Spencer, for example, and also by McDonald's.

Although the Department of Education and Science has recommended that all pupils should receive at least part of their final school certificate in the form of a profiled record of achievement, this will be in addition to examination in the formal curriculum. Profiling of the new pre-vocational curriculum is typically seen as giving credit to pupils who are not expected to do well in orthodox examinations by acknowledging informal learning outside the classroom. 'Profiling', claimed one enthusiast quoted in *The Times Educational Supplement*, 'can assess, say, the learning gained by helping to care for younger brothers and sisters, or helping to run a Saturday market stall.' What is missing from this image of achievement is any notion of improving the level of students' powers. The concern is merely to record ever more carefully an increasing number and kinds of success. This begins to approach Ivan Illich's nightmare vision of the 'universal classroom', where every human activity is scrutinised and validated by the institutions of formal education!

The same criticism can be made of the Joint Board's Certificate of Pre-Vocational Education. This was the main record of achievement in this area before it was eclipsed by the emphasis now placed upon the traditionally academic National Curriculum. CPVE was intended for the 'new sixth form' of non-academic school returners who were anticipated in the schools and FE colleges as youth unemployment rose. As has been seen, it was also planned as the certificate of YTS completion. Although CPVE was presented as suitable for a wide range of ability, its academic standards were not very high. An HMI report which welcomed the CPVE as 'a valuable opportunity for students to discover or confirm their vocational orientation' also cautioned, 'many students move from the CPVE into courses, training or employment for which they might appear to have been qualified a year earlier. [So] it is necessary for institutions to evaluate carefully the benefits which individual students gain by devoting a year to the CPVE.'

CPVE was pre-vocational in its division into a core of ten subjects, such as numeracy and information technology, but it then attempted, rather like YTS, to move on to more specifically vocational studies. In a kind of one-year careers education programme 'vocational studies' focused students' occupational aspirations together with work experience and induction into one of five employment categories. These were then subdivided into narrower work clusters. Instead of the traditional two-year subject courses for GCSE and A-level examination, the one-year CPVE was broken down into a series of modules. Each of these learning units could be completed in the six to eight weeks of a half term. Again, these were divided into introductory and exploratory modules allowing students to try different work activities. Finally, preparatory modules primed students or YTS trainees for a particular occupation. Extra modules were designed to make the CPVE fit with other courses of study, or used for 'community activities, leisure, recreation and reflection'.

Modules are not 'a sequential division of the curriculum', as the Further Education Unit explained, but 'a series of free-standing learning objectives with "build up" effect': in other words, a module can stand alone or form part of a route picked through the various units on offer. In the NVQ modules the intention is for the practical competencies and theoretical knowledge demonstrated in each unit to offer the possibility of further progression. For as long as certain core areas are covered, students can choose different combinations to suit their individual abilities and interests. This approach has been familiar for a long time in American degree courses, where building blocks from different disciplines are combined, for instance using bits of literature, art appreciation and history to form 'Renaissance Studies'. They are similarly used by the Open University, where self-study allows a flexibility of individual approaches.

At this higher education level, the danger of such a student-centred approach is that any sense of such coherent disciplines as traditions of knowledge and enquiry is lost. The boundaries between many disciplines are notoriously irrational and ill-defined, however, and new disciplines often arise from sharing the perspectives of old ones. But they do not necessarily just spring fully-armed from following the majority choice of students across the range of available units. With tuition and support, however, the unique contributions of the various disciplines can be both preserved and combined. This dilemma is clearer at the lower level of general pre-vocational courses, where the modules that are chosen need be related only by their practical similarities and to the vocational aspirations of the student. The theoretical relation of one area to another as part of a whole can therefore be lost in favour of practical application to particular tasks which are not necessarily related to one another. There must always be opportunities to make the connection of how the part relates to the whole; also for progression from one level to another, as is intended by the NCVQ, so that students are given opportunities beyond just collecting a selection of the lower-level modules.

The modular approach implies a new relationship between teacher and pupil, in that learning is understood as problem-solving rather than simply memorising information. This involves abandoning the 'teacher paradigm' whereby students gave authority to the teacher in exchange for information. Instead, teachers and students together negotiate the best learning approaches: rather than just imparting 'the facts', the teaching role becomes that of enabling this process to occur.

The increased element of choice can also enhance student motivation, and offer a means to update and add to existing courses. In traditionally divided subjects additional modules can cover some of the many pre-vocational elements now required of society's new citizens. This modular approach survives in some GCSEs, where it affords one way to prepare previously streamed and segregated students for a unitary exam. Modular divisions of the curriculum also facilitate supported self-study. For older students, like Open University undergraduates, this involves unsupervised private study, distance learning through various media, off-site working, some collaborative learning, and essential but not necessarily frequent tutorial support. With the continuing shortage of teachers, this 'distance learning' may also become more common in many schools.

In fact, the full positive implications of a modular curriculum are unlikely to be realised in schools under the traditional subject divisions which make up the National Curriculum. Some of the negative potential of modular courses becomes apparent at the lower and more general level of pre-vocational courses like CPVE. This course, which was supported by a coalition of examining boards, is at least not so narrowly confined solely to what employers require of new recruits as are some of the certificates devised by other single exam boards. The Royal Society of Arts' clerical Voc Prep course, for example, lists as the 'Behavioural Objective' required of students under its 'career and personal development' topic 'To appreciate the attitudes and expectations of employers'. The Associated Examinating Board has gone further in designing an exam explicitly to save employers the time and expense of screening recruits by giving them tests in basic maths and English.

'It is enormously time consuming and expensive for commercial and industrial firms to give aptitude tests to 400 or 500 applicants at a time... There is an immediate advantage if young people can take tests of this sort in school twice a year and the results can be made available to employers', stated the AEB's development officer. Pre-vocational education has here reverted to its nineteenth-century board school worst.

However bad things become, they can always get worse. A project conducted by the Social and Psychological Research Unit at Sheffield University assessed the skills required for 'starting work' and compiled a list of 'very important skills'. These included: 'Bend, stretch or reach; Finger, hand, wrist speed; Push, pull or carry heavy objects; Manual dexterity'. At least the turn towards assessing retention of irrelevant academic 'facts' has spared teachers from carrying out such 'work-related' time and motion studies on their pupils.

Further education

The changes that were introduced by vocational education and training have so far been examined mainly in the context of schools, where they affected the largest numbers of people; but in many ways they went deepest in the further education sector of education. This presently comprises 1.75 million full- and part-time students and it is extraordinary that it is not more often a focus of educational attention, especially as many of the changes that later spread to the rest of education were first introduced in this sector. It really deserves a book to itself but it will be looked at briefly here in the context of the part it plays in the vocational education and training which it has influenced so much.

The 400 FE colleges have been described as the heirs to the *ad hoc* mixture of self-improvement, government training centres and employer need for more theoretically proficient technicians in science-based industries, like electronics and chemicals. As the successors to Mechanics Institutes and night schools and the base for day-release from apprenticeship, technical colleges doubled in number during the war to take some 200,000 full- and part-time students. Unlike other state training efforts, they were not abandoned after the war but doubled in numbers again to train over 400,000 part-time employees by 1957.

The Ministry of Education endorsed a confident *Future Development of Higher Technological Education* for what it described as these 'unique institutions ... Certainly not to be found either in the United States of America or most countries on the Continent of Europe, whereby young people entering industry at the age of 15 or 16 have been able to continue their education concurrently with the discipline and experience of work.'

Education and training took place in the colleges away from the place of work, even though standards were set by employer and professional bodies. The London Livery Companies, for instance, established the City and Guilds of London Institute to regulate standards nationally through technical examinations. More recently, separate Business and Technician Education Councils were set up and merged in 1984 to form BTEC.

CGLI and BTEC were the main qualifications that FE had prepared its students for in the past. But even between these two and the other main examining body, the Royal Society of Arts, qualifications were based on different levels from Part 1 to licentiate, first to Higher National and then in stages, none of which corresponded to each other. The various qualifications served overlapping purposes and often reflected different ideas about education; they were not compatible in sequence, standards or structure. This variety of different routes set by over 300 different awarding bodies resulted in what Sir Keith (now Lord) Joseph, when he was Education

Minister, called 'a bewildering variety of courses with a multitude of strange initials'. It was one of the major weaknesses of Britain's vocational education and training identified by the Review of Vocational Qualifications which recommended the standardisation now being attempted by the NCVQ. Already, a NVQ database allows comparison across the range of qualifications in all occupational areas and at different levels of competence. Transfer is not yet so easy, except in terms of whole qualifications.

The original concentration of the colleges upon (male) day-release apprentices widened progressively. For a start, more and more (female) office workers began to come into FE as that sector of the economy expanded, and the majority of FE students are now women (54 per cent).

During the 1970s, rather than stay on at school as had been anticipated, the 'new sixth form' of unemployed school-leavers gravitated instead towards the more adult atmosphere of their local FE college. Here they joined what had always been a service provided by FE of giving orientation and support to special school-leavers with moderate or severe learning difficulties. 'Multi-skills' workshops, originally used with special schools groups, have suddenly proliferated in the colleges where, supervised by the interdisciplinary teams of lecturers, trainees practise a little cookery, joinery, housecraft, mend plugs, replace fuses and learn other 'life skills'. In addition, there is repeated emphasis upon the core areas of literacy, numeracy and keyboard skills. This became known as the new tertiary modern FE.

When YTS came along, these courses were converted to schemes in exchange for the grant of £1,950 which the MSC initially awarded to managing agents for every trainee they enrolled. But although they had better facilities than many of the shoestring operators who presented themselves as private managing agents, the colleges were tied to term-times and criticised for not responding enough to employers' demands upon YTS. They were forced into an unequal competition with the large employer-based schemes which at least offered the possibility of employment to their trainees.

With the demographic fall in demand, many schemes on employers' premises reverted to employee status and 'topped up' the training allowance towards wage levels. Some local authority-run schemes have always managed to do this as a matter of principle, but the colleges were not in a good position to compete. They were left with the Mode B 1 and 2 schemes, as they were called, for their special needs youngsters and other 'disadvantaged' youth.

On other courses that actually impart marketable skills, trainees are better off converting to student status whereby they can enjoy the benefits of term-time hours and holidays, even though their educational maintenance allowance is less than the Training Allowance. (That is, if they can get an EMA, which is a discretionary award by the local authority for most FE courses.)

At one time the Manpower Services Commission threatened to take over all non-advanced further education, as it used to be called, by assuming direct control of its £220 million funding. A compromise arrangement means that the Department of Employment's Training Agency, as the once independent MSC has now become, collaborates with the colleges to plan and administer these NAFE courses.

Changes in funding for the two-year YTS reduced the subsidy available for Mode B, subsequently called Premium, schemes. The redirection of YTS towards employers' premises was in any case always the government's intention, so the substantial part played by the colleges in the launch of YTS was something of a stopgap. Apart from some surviving Premium, or Category B, schemes, the colleges have, as far as YT is concerned, largely reverted to their previous role of servicing apprenticeships, now redesignated YT.

To deal with the influx of new recruits to FE, student-centred approaches to learning were pioneered by lecturers who recast themselves as 'facilitators' and 'managers of the learning process' rather than 'information dispensers', as BTEC put it. This was often difficult for staff who had spent many years previously teaching third-year apprentice plumbers, for instance, to suddenly impart the 'transferable skills' of first-year YTS. When these new courses hardly enjoy parity of esteem and security of employment with traditional FE studies, practical or academic, there is resistance to forfeiting a teaching role in order to become course administrators and educational technicians. Nor has the avalanche of change that has fallen upon FE yet passed. If the NCVQ's proposals for a competence-based curriculum go ahead, one study of their implications estimated, 'In terms of the numbers of staff who will be directly affected over the next 3 or 4 years, this will have greater impact than the impact of BTEC, YTS and CPVE combined'.

Profiling and modular assessments were introduced, both as ways to break down previous craft courses into digestible units for the new type of student and to increase motivation which was often lacking, and to establish flexible control over a fluid situation. The new vocationalism, as it came to be called, was developed in the FE colleges, building upon school link courses that already brought students out of their classrooms into the college workshops. The scheme was supported by a Further Education Unit set up in the Department of Education in 1977 which employed a 'cascade model' of curriculum-led staff development to quickly spread its gospel of experiential learning through participation – learning by doing. The FEU's influence upon the subsequent spread of vocational education in training schemes and schools cannot be underestimated, both as a 'Trojan horse' for the Manpower Services Commission inside the DES, and the source for many of the MSC's educational ideas. This influence is perhaps most marked in the case of new types of assessment. Instead of end-of-course examinations, formative assessment as part of the learning process aims not to fail students but to teach them to learn from their mistakes. To do this they have to communicate with their tutor who is also their assessor. The process is student-centred rather than pre-set by the course syllabus for examination. An action plan may be established as the first stage of deciding upon a negotiated curriculum with a more or less formal contract between learner and facilitator setting out what they aim to achieve and how they will go about it.

As with the selection of modular options, counselling of the student at regular intervals allows progress to be reviewed and recorded. Self-assessment, assessment on demand and assessment by fellow students may also form part of group work on an assignment or module that will be assessed. The claims to objectivity of this kind of assessment rest upon the criterion of whether or not students are competent to actually do what they are being tested on, rather than just to write about it. They demonstrate what they have learnt in the real situations in which they will need to use them at work.

As well as being squeezed from below by the vastly expanded pre-vocational courses, traditional vocational craft and clerical courses in FE colleges have also been squeezed from above by academic A-level classes for students from comprehensives which have lost their sixth forms. The trend towards tertiary colleges combining sixth-form centres with FE colleges puts these three distinct tiers of students under one roof. Each tier follows a separate route of study with contrasted teaching styles, methods of assessment and course content.

The future of these 55 tertiary colleges must be as uncertain as everything else following the passage of the Education Reform Act. It will be very difficult for local authorities to create any more of them by rationalising secondary schools into consortia that share sixth form facilities, although Sheffield is attempting to do so. Any school threatened with the loss of its sixth form can now vote to opt out of local authority control and, given the Secretary of State's approval, maintain itself on grants from central government. This can only entrench the belief, inherited from the grammar schools, that a good sixth form lies at the heart of a good school, even though the elitism and excessive academic specialisation of A levels has been widely condemned from the point of view of any vocational relevance. It also reinforces the now outdated, middle-class notion of FE colleges as places where other people go to learn a trade. Yet the association of different levels of study in tertiary colleges could at least facilitate transfer between them in order to increase access.

Like the NCVQ framework, the new forms of assessment first piloted in FE and the experiential learning-by-doing are intended to facilitate access and enable transition from one level to another. FE colleges also pioneered access courses to higher education. Open Colleges link FE and adult education course provision with universities and polytechnics to encourage non-standard entry to higher education, mostly by mature students.

A federation of Open Colleges, based at Northern College, Barnsley, is working with the Council for National Academic Awards to create a framework for access to higher education courses. Their 'learning passports' offer a means to credit and accumulate previously unrecognised experience and unsystematised knowledge. Sensitive counselling and tuition aims to overcome the problems faced by adult learners while addressing their concerns and enabling them to make contributions to the body of subject knowledge they are studying. Unfortunately the financial problems of unemployed students have been considerably added to lately by the change in benefit rules that previously allowed part-time study on the dole for up to 21 hours a week.

The MSC attempted to build on the success of the Open Colleges by promoting its own 'Open College of the Air', but this failed to meet its targets for enrolment because its courses, run at commercial rates, were too expensive. Its critics called it the Open College in the Air! Consequently, the renamed Open College has moved towards company work, devising programmes of training which are customised for particular employers' purposes. There is also an Open College of the Arts which aims to help people of all and any ages to learn arts and crafts in their own homes. This was sponsored, not by the former MSC supremo Lord Young of Graffham, but by Lord Young of Dartington.

Efforts by the MSC and other quangos, such as the London Docklands Development Corporation, to establish 'skills passports' (though the NVQ may become such) and to make education and training available through 'drop-in centres' and even 'skills supermarkets', have so far had an air of gimmickry about them. They are too unsystematic and too responsive to limited, immediate demands from individuals to have any credibility as worthwhile additions to skills or experience.

The Open Tech, launched by the MSC in 1983, largely funded an expansion of distance-learning schemes and materials. The National Extension College provides a directory to technical courses with are intended to complement the academic courses of the Open University. Like the OU, some of these courses have begun to develop the potential of information technology to link tutors and students via Prestel and Telecom Gold, as well as posted learning packages, videos, tapes, telephone conferences, television and radio programmes. However, the most effective form of information technology for such supported self-study – interactive video on laser disc – is still too expensive for widespread use.

Despite all the influence and innovation that can be attributed to the further education sector, and the FE colleges in particular, these were not spared in the 1988 reform of education, as the colleges were judged to have been still not responsive enough to employers' needs. This accusation is always peculiarly irksome to college staff, because their colleges arose out of such a response and the courses in them have always evolved in consultation with local industry and commerce. Yet the Act gives reserve powers to the Secretary of State to extend the National Curriculum for schools to further education from 16 to 19 (and to non-university higher education), and these powers could be used to make the colleges more responsive to industrial demand.

At the heart of the new plans is a core curriculum of the 'three Rs'; personal relations; and familiarity with new technology and 'the world of work', especially the need for 'flexibility' in changing work and social contexts. While this pre-vocational curriculum would cover what is already being done in some areas of FE provision, it does not match the variety of courses on offer. Nor would it accord with the competence-based curriculum of the NCVQ any more than would the National Curriculum in schools. However, it might help to bring people back into education, even later in life, if it were presented as a minimum 'entitlement curriculum'. For such an option to be a reality for many people, they would have to be adequately sustained on study grants and/or have the right to attend college while working without loss of pay.

Such an 'entitlement curriculum' is not perhaps uppermost in the government's thinking. Rather, a National Curriculum will enable it to keep control of what goes on in the colleges when they, like the rest of education, are cut loose from local authority control – 'towards independence', as junior Education Minister Angela Rumbold put it. From being primarily course-producers, colleges will change to being forced to sell to survive a wider range of consultancy services, such as training needs analysis, assessment support, production of open learning materials, etc.

Like the schools, the FE colleges will have to compete with each other for dwindling numbers of students in the open education market-place. College governing bodies, beefed up with a minimum 50 per cent of employers' representatives, are charged with wide-ranging, major powers. Employers' representatives cannot include those of the local authority itself, even though the local Council has long been the major employer in many areas.

The model seems to be that of the American community colleges with their small governing bodies. Business interests indicated to the government during the passage of the Education Reform bill that they would be hard-pressed to whip up the numbers for the larger bodies originally envisaged: no more than 25 members are now stipulated, with as few as ten recommended. Beneath them it can be expected that the Principal of the college will no longer be both chief executive and leading professional chairperson of the academic board. Instead, rather like a football team manager, he (typically) will be a business manager, hiring and firing staff at local rather than national rates. Success in running the business at a profit will determine whether the Principal's rolling contract will be renewed by the board. In the USA, this insecurity of tenure is at least compensated for by company perks, such as cars, insurance and private health policies and travel allowances for spouses.

While the local authority still has an important planning and monitoring role, employers' representatives and others on the new governing bodies will make all the decisions. These are likely to be in the direction of what is immediately required and can be profitably sold to local industry and commerce. Coherent programmes of vocational education and training will be degraded if there is such a concentration on narrower, job-specific skills. 'Roll-on roll-off' courses are envisaged with students choosing individualised packages from a menu of core and option choices in a 'pick-'n-mix' arrangement.

The relationship of academic boards (which decide on the educational content of courses in colleges) to the new governing bodies is unclear; but, as an FEU commentary on the new arrangements ominously concluded, 'Some rationalisation and a reduction in lecturer numbers seems inevitable'.

The part played by the colleges in providing further education for students with special educational needs is safeguarded by section 120 of the Education Reform Act, but the Act makes no mention of adult education. Adult learners are included under the umbrella term 'Further Education'. This is now clearly separated from 'Higher Education' and from post-compulsory education which does not provide a significant amount of part-time education, e.g. sixth-form colleges. Sixty per cent of FE students are over 19; in addition, there are 1,600,000 mainly part-time students attending adult education institutes.

The structural separation of further from higher education will make it much more difficult to sustain the partnerships upon which depend access courses to HE for adults through FE. A coherent adult training and retraining strategy, which was one of the original aims of the 1981 New Training Initiative, will be rendered difficult, if not impossible, by the likely marginalisation of adult continuing education. This accounted for only 0.5 per cent of local authority education spending in 1989, excepting the ILEA, which spent 2 per cent of its budget on London's adult education institutes.

The demographic fall in the numbers of 16–19-year-olds will reach its trough in 1994, and to make up their numbers it has been estimated that colleges will need an extra million enrolments. But, according to a survey made by the Training Commission (what the MSC briefly became before it was further downgraded to Training Agency), employers are beginning to take on 16-year-olds again. They seem oblivious to the needs of a national training policy and the goal of constructing a coherent programme of transition from school to work which has been so emphasised over the past decade and more. Certainly, it can hardly be in the long-term interest of the economy or of young people themselves if even more of them are being attracted away from full-time education and training schemes.

Higher education

Like the further education sector, higher education is beyond the scope of this brief survey of vocational education and training. In general terms however, the higher you progress up the education system the more specifically vocational education becomes, as it is more directly linked to employment and, moreover, to some specific employment.

This is clearly the case for courses in subjects with specific technical applications like engineering or architecture, or those that are limited in their occupational application, like accountancy or law. But even then, while private companies may sponsor students through their courses in the expectation of employing them for a guaranteed period on completion, it is rare for the course to be so job-specific as to tie the graduate to one particular employment. The most specialised courses still aim to cover the entire field of study, if not in detail at least in outline.

Many higher education courses, while subject-specific, are not vocationally specific: some courses that mix different fields of study are not even subject-specific. Indeed, as the great French educational sociologist Emile Durkheim observed, the only specific vocational function of higher education courses is to reproduce the academics who run them. The range of possible occupations for which they qualify is large, not only because a degree is a high-level qualification encompassing many lower levels, but because, while most graduates start their careers in a named function – like finance, personnel or engineering – employers expect them to move quickly into management positions. The trend in recent years has been for more occupations that aspire to professional status to become closed to applicants without degrees. So completing higher education has likewise tended to become confirmation of professional/managerial, or, even more loosely, 'middle-class' status.

Whatever the actual subject of study, higher education courses convey the social attitudes and abilities required of professional-level workers. In this sense they are pre-vocational, but to a higher level than the pre-vocational preparation for all occupations provided for 16-year-old school-leavers.

More specifically vocational courses may be required on top of the degree: for instance, the one-year teacher training or social work diploma, followed by periods of probation in the profession with additional specialisation as part of professional training.

An ever-widening range of organisations is now seeking to recruit graduates and demand is rising annually: by the early 1990s graduate output will peak, although demand for graduates will still increase, and it is predicted that output will not recover until the year 2000. Moreover, there are shortages in key economic areas such as physics and engineering, while student applications are falling for science and engineering, technology, physics, modern languages and maths and rising for humanities, social science and business and administration. This is the case even though graduate unemployment rates are highest for arts subjects (around 10 per cent compared with around 7 per cent for all subjects in 1987). In addition, there is a celebrated 'brain drain', not only to the USA but also, more substantially, to the other countries of the European Community (17,700 professional and managerial workers left for the Continent against only 5,200 coming in during 1986).

These are not very encouraging signs for those seeking to bring higher education into line with the demands of the economy in the same way that the rest of the education system was vocationalised from 1976 to 1987. The Manpower Services Commission had long regarded higher education as ripe for rationalisation, notwithstanding, or perhaps because of, the fact that most academics thought the initials MSC stood for a type of higher degree.

In 1987 a £100 million Enterprise in Higher Education Initiative was announced, and eleven institutions, individually or in consortia, were chosen from all those which bid for £200,000 each over the next five years. In return they would undertake 'to develop competencies and aptitudes relevant to enterprise' in all their students. A further thirteen have since been approved and similar numbers are supposed to come 'on-stream' in each succeeding year. The EHEI was announced as TVEI for higher education and, like TVEI, government money was intended only to set up the scheme. After their initial five years, enterprise programmes should become self-financing; or rather, funded by enterprise itself in the shape of local businessmen. For this reason, bids for the first hand-out had to include 'a contribution from employers in cash or in kind equivalent to at least 25 per cent of the MSC contri-bution over the first two years and rising to a substantial proportion of the programme from the third year of the programme'.

The term 'in cash or in kind' provided a let-out for the employers whom the college authorities hurriedly approached; thus they did not actually have to put up the money immediately but could instead offer old equipment or the use of their premises for students on work placements, or visits as payment in kind. Intercalary years, industrial visits and work experience are already common on many undergraduate courses, and Brunel University has even built all its courses around them. Polytechnics in particular have always had close working relations with employers, sandwich-course degrees and often a more practical approach to learning. However, as with the schools–industry Compacts, it may be that some companies will now become involved in the EHEI in order to ensure their future supplies of student recruits.

The aim of the Initiative is that 'every person seeking a higher education qualification should be able to develop competencies and aptitudes relevant to enterprise'. 'Enterprise', admits the Training Agency's characteristically glossy brochure, 'is a buzzword.' Or, as *The Times Higher Education Supplement* commented on EHEI's launch, 'a richly ambiguous concept'.

According to a study of the development of EHEI, enterprise was at first defined in an entrepreneurial sense of business skills: modules merely bolted-on to existing academic courses were thus proposed which were aimed at increasing student awareness of business. This narrow approach soon broadened into the idea of encouraging work placements and project-based work to be carried out in an economic environment. Some departments, notably education, were already undertaking such studies with, in addition, student-assessed learning and negotiated contracts. Finally, the definition of enterprise settled upon an emphasis on personal transferable skills.

'The core skills of an enterprising person that lie at the heart of an enterprising culture' are already familiar from many previous vocationally relevant programmes in education: 'The workplace of today and tomorrow requires employees who are resourceful and flexible and can adapt quickly to changes in the nature of their skills and knowledge. They will be able to innovate, recognise and create opportunities, work in a team, take risks and respond to challenges, communicate effectively and be computer literate.'

These are the pre-vocational skills now required of higher-level managerial and administrative professional workers by a 'demand-flexible' environment that requires them to train and retrain throughout working life. For academics this implies, familiarly, that 'staff become "facilitators" rather than teachers' and courses become even more student-centred than they are already. Staff development is therefore a leading element in EHE schemes.

'Initial higher education should emphasise underlying principles ... [including] the ability to analyse complex issues, to identify the core of the problem ... to synthesise ... to work co-operatively and constructively with others and ... to communicate clearly.' This definition by the National Advisory Body on Public Sector Higher Education of the professional pre-vocational skills imparted by HE gains the Training Agency's approval as also covering 'enterprise skills'.

The Training Agency has been fairly explicit about its view of the EHEI's place in the overall strategy for the reform of higher education. It intends to make the system more open in order to encourage flexibility and progression, and in the case of higher education this ideal is rendered necessary by the fall in numbers of young people. It means that the universities and polytechnics will have both to compete for dwindling numbers of students and allow open access to adults and more non-academically qualified entrants. This aim is, of course, at variance with the introduction of a loan or voucher system to pay the full fees which students will now be charged, and which will surely restrict the access of wider numbers of people to higher education. Similarly, the powers of direction which the government has assumed over funding courses towards those judged to make a contribution to economic growth contradicts the powers of choice supposedly given to the individual consumer of education services (student).

Nevertheless, the writing is clearly on the wall for the traditional three-year finishing course as the accepted transition from school to work for middle-class youth. Instead, shorter courses, which the MSC piloted long ago in certain polytechnics, with modularised courses awarding credits for transfer to different institutions and working longer terms, if not all year round, are all on the cards. In this new world, the enterprise skills of selling services on a contractual basis are, as the Training Agency points out, increasingly necessary for higher education itself to fund courses and research.

Meanwhile, rather than seeking to prepare the ground for such fundamental changes but now dovetailing with them, a more modest government programme of £13 million a year has, since 1982, been providing specialist short courses in practical skills required by professionals in their changing work. This Professional, Industrial and Commercial Updating is supplied to nearly one million adults annually by colleges of further and higher education. Initially, PICKUP was seen as being particularly relevant to the needs of industry for training in the new technology, but 'continuing professional development' is now recognised as necessary for all professional workers in a rapidly changing world. The scheme emanated from the Department of Education and Science rather than the Manpower Services Commission (as was), where most other training and vocational initiatives originated and where the bulk of government funding went. Perhaps because of this, PICKUP never developed the same high profile as did other initiatives, but it is undoubtedly more effective than many of them.

There is also a European Community Programme for Education and Training for Technology (COMETT) which aims to give a European dimension to co-operation between universities and enterprises in training related to the development and application of new technology. Like Enterprise in Higher Education, this also seeks to establish University–Enterprise Training Partnerships (UETPs). Like the European Community Action Scheme for the Mobility of University Students (ERASMUS) between different higher education institutions, COMETT sponsors transnational exchanges between colleges and firms in different EC countries.

The Open University has also been involved, since it was founded more than twenty years ago, in Career Development for Professionals (CDP). Indeed, at one time the majority of its part-time, adult students were teachers upgrading their certificates to degrees. The OU based its approach upon the distance learning that has become so popular for the flexible provision of vocational education and training courses. The corollary of this approach was a pedagogical practice of 'open learning'. At its core is a multi-media package of student-centred learning resources including written texts, television, radio and, more recently, computers. Packages are devised by course teams, with great attention being paid to providing the opportunity for self-assessment by students. Support for the work comes from tutors who provide feedback by correspondence or in meetings at local study centres and residential schools.

As its name implies, the Open University places no bar on access to its courses; students are accepted on a first-come, first-served basis. The range of occupational interests has extended, as has the large number of students who follow courses purely for their own personal development, e.g. retired people. The heavy balance in favour of men in the early years has swung from 73 to 45 per cent, so that the majority of students are now women and most students are in the 26–40 age-range, although the age limit for entry has been dropped from 25 to 21. Total student numbers stand at 60,000 undergraduates and 40,000 continuing education students, including post-graduates.

Unlike the Open College and the new loan system for all higher education, OU students are not expected to be self-financing. Their contributions do not cover the total costs of their courses although there is constant pressure for them to do so and some fees have recently been increased. However, continuing education for professionals in such areas as health and welfare, business studies, accountancy and science enables the OU to adequately support its open learning.

For the open and student-centred learning, to which it has been seen all the new vocational education and training aspires, does not come cheap if it is done properly. It aims to remove all obstacles to learning so that students work at their own pace in their own way and time and with the learning resources appropriate to attain their own goals. This process begins with a recognition of the students' personal circumstances and the stage of learning they have reached, which is then used to determine the advice and counselling they need and the design of their learning programmes. Progression is achieved through the modular approaches which have become familiar. Students assemble their own programmes of study from the range of options available that match their past attainments and their present needs and interests. Counselling them within the disciplines of various academic approaches is therefore the crucial element of the tutor's task. Course design is also critical to success, especially where project work is involved; unless courses are carefully structured and have strong tutorial backup, students tend to drop out.

Such open learning is the means to achieve the goal of continuing vocational education and training throughout working life. Modular courses are necessary to foster collaborative programmes between different levels of education and to allow access to them. The national validation of vocational and professional qualifications that is planned by the NCVQ means that a student should be able to accumulate a number of credits with the same vocational value from a number of different institutions. These courses should be full- or part-time to meet the personal circumstances of different students with a variety of needs.

Yet training courses which result in limited vocational outcomes are not educational because they do not lead on to further opportunities for development; neither are they useful vocationally because in order to act to greatest effect with the newest technology, workers need a much wider range of knowledge and skills than those required for only one specific job. Thus, in the words of Professor John Bynner from the Open University, 'Open Learning must be seen as opening many more doors than those leading just to employment'.

European comparisons: West Germany and Scotland

West Germany

There are definite fashions in the foreign models held out for emulation by an ailing British economy. For a long time Sweden was the promised land of social reform and good labour relations. The original model of the Manpower Services Commission, first proposed by the TUC, was the Swedish Manpower Board. This combined comprehensive training and manpower planning with an incomes policy that had wide political appeal.

With the eclipse of social democracy in England and a Christian Democrat government in the Federal Republic, West Germany replaced its Nordic neighbour as the model for economic success. Lately, however, the USA seems to have succeeded Germany as the ideal of a more enterprising economy. The MSC's 1984 comparative study *Competence and Competition* was influential in contrasting the investment in training made by Germany, Japan and the USA with that made in the UK.

It is easy to see why West Germany appeals to English educationalists and trainers alike. Its federal system of education and training is locally administered by the regional governments, just as the English and Welsh education system was by local government until recently. The tripartite system of state schools is also familiar to the UK from the 1944 Education Act, but it is not such a closed system as was British tripartite schooling.

All state primaries are non-selective, except by the residential area which they serve; however, teachers allocate pupils to appropriate secondaries on the basis of a series of regular tests. Despite the public esteem in which German teachers are generally held, parental appeal is possible and quite often successful so that transfer is feasible from the secondary modern Hauptschule to the largely technical Realschule and the grammar-type Gymnasium. In theory too, but less often in actuality, transfer and progression is also open in the post-school system between universities, the equivalent of polytechnics, higher trade and technical colleges, apprentice-ship and adult education.

The main attraction to British teachers and trainers is that the German system succeeds in providing meaningful qualification to over 90 per cent of its school-leavers. There is not such a complete parting of the ways at 16 as there is in England and Wales. Instead, a large proportion of young people remain in education or in vocational education and training until age 18 or 19. The result is, as Her Majesty's Inspectors of schools recorded on a visit to two contrasted States of the FRG, 'The "bottom 40 per cent", as they are sometimes called here, are not, in the German system, sealed into that position by curriculum and age cut-offs'.

It was the 'dual system' of apprenticeship that particularly interested British teachers and trainers. Full-time education is only compulsory in the Federal Republic from age 6 to 16, sometimes 15. But subsequently, for those under age 18 who are not in the top 25 per cent continuing their studies to the A-level equivalent of Abitur, part-time education at a school which we would call a further education college is compulsory for one or two days a week (generally two). Thus by law, all young people receive some kind of liberal or vocational education until the age of 18.

This statutory attendance forms part of two- to 3½-year apprenticeships in some 400 recognised trades. Main school (but not intermediate and Gymnasium) pupils are given help and advice in finding these apprenticeships by careers advisers from the local jobcentres as part of a programme of work-learning. However, school-leavers have to make their own applications and employers make their own selections, on which basis a legally binding contract is drawn up. This is more like the old apprentice's indentureship to his employer than the statements of good intentions embodied in 'contracts' between pupils and local employers in British and American Compact schemes. Young workers may work full-time only if their firms provide training in-house (which most large companies do). Alternatively, youngsters can attend full-time technical education courses. Most follow the dual track route of practical work in their firm and related education at college.

Much of the educational component is general and theoretical, and includes subjects like German, mathematics and social studies. This resembles the old liberal studies for apprentices in FE colleges, only to a higher level and for inclusion in examination. There is a probationary period to apprenticeship, followed by interim and final examinations, the latter comprising theoretical, practical, oral and written sections. Apprentices may retake their finals three times, and ultimately over 90 per cent pass. As between theory and practice, between education and work it is the workplace that is of central importance.

This system is jointly controlled by the state, employers and trade unions and is funded mainly by employers through a levy on all firms, whether they train or not. Like the apprenticeship system in Britain, the dual system evolved from medieval craftsmen's guilds, but this was only achieved in the 1920s when compulsory attendance at vocational schools was introduced. With the reconstruction of German industry after the war, the system was legally regularised in a series of reforms during the 1960s and 1970s.

The comprehensive vocational training law (Berufs-bildungsgesetz/BBiG) gives force to the articles of apprenticeship and the contract between apprentices and their employers. It also recognises the trades running the apprenticeship schemes; firms are not compelled to provide training, but if they do it must follow the existing training regulations. Professional associations also conduct specialised training for their different occupations. Apprentices who complete their training are not guaranteed employment, but they do acquire recognised qualifications which give them rights to minimum remuneration in that employment, guaranteed social insurance (for example, a disability pension) and an entitlement to further subsidised training or retraining. Like YT, apprenticeship is compulsory in that anyone choosing not to enter it loses claim to social aid, except in exceptional circumstances. Unlike YT in many cases, apprenticeship is the first and not the last resort of German school-leavers.

Nor is apprenticeship qualification as a bachelor the end of a tradesman's career, as further practical and theoretical examination can lead to a mastership. This examination, taken at around the age of 30, requires demonstration not only of advanced occupational knowledge but also of pedagogical and managerial competence. Study for it thus involves not only production of a master work but also instruction and practice in the obligation to train further apprentices. The role of the *Meister* in the dual system is therefore pivotal, as without a qualified master it is not possible to run many businesses. For example, you cannot make and sell bread unless there is a master baker in the bakery.

This touches upon one of the fundamental cultural differences between the two countries. Although the German system is a hierarchic and bureaucratic one, there is not the same cultural distinction made between professions and trades as in Britain. In fact, the word *Beruf* incorporates all the meanings covered by the English terms occupation, vocation (in its original sense of calling), profession and trade.

There is always a danger that in abstracting the formal structure of another country's way of doing things, that country's cultural context is left behind; thus we may never really understand the meaning that they have for the people who live in that context. For instance, the principle in Germany that school-leaving certificates give absolute entitlement to the next stage of education or training rests upon the attendant system of pupils repeating a year that they fail at school. (More rarely, school students may also skip a year ahead.) The marks upon which some 20 per cent of German youngsters are forced to do this every year (often with considerable protest from themselves and their parents) are scaled along six points from 'sehr gut' to 'very poor'. The German system, with its internal examinations and continuous assessment, leaves considerable scope for the teacher.

In Germany, school education after age 16 is general, rather than occupationally or academically specific. Unlike the narrowly specialist A levels, entrants to higher education must combine subjects from three broad areas of study – language and the arts, maths and science, plus social studies. Their three years of study for the Abitur entitling them to university entrance also include at least two foreign languages. Upon this generalist base the higher education institutions are more vocationally specific than is the case in Britain. As well as the universities, there is a hierarchy of technical, teacher-training and Civil Service colleges, music and art schools and higher technical schools. These last provide practice-related courses with a scientific or artistic base, particularly in the fields of engineering, economics, social science, agriculture and design. In addition, there are comprehensive universities combining these various roles into integrated studies which are open to students with different school-leaving and training certificates. Nearly 20 per cent of those over age 16 continue with some form of higher education, compared with 12.5 per cent in Britain, and this percentage is increasing in the FRG. Courses of study are longer, ranging from four to six years. It is however a very academic system, and the binary divide between the universities and the other higher education institutions is wider than in the UK.

It is the same in Japan, where students pursue a general education to a high if rather theoretical level without any particular practical application and even more young people remain in education to a later age. The Japanese system is also sometimes recommended for imitation by Britain but, to Brits who so notably lack the Japanese facility for learning from others, its remote culture renders it incomprehensible.

Like Japan's extended education system, Germany's is also expensive. Her Majesty's Inspectors noted approvingly the 'high-cost system of expensively trained and well-paid teachers working in high-quality and well-maintained buildings, and teaching carefully developed curricula in which much time, money and corporate effort have been invested'.

The adequate funding of training by a levy upon employers is similarly regarded with envy by Britain's training community. The Industrial Training Boards to which some employers paid a levy to co-ordinate apprenticeships were disbanded with characteristic brusqueness during Norman Tebbit's reign at the Department of Employment. The fact that British employers are notoriously reluctant to pay for education or training which they do not directly require has been noted, and it is unlikely that they will be any more forthcoming under the new Training and Enterprise Councils which they now control. Britain's employers should not be singled out for blame in this regard, however. Although their reluctance to train has been repeatedly noted, they are no more or less 'greedy' and 'shortsighted' than their German and Japanese counterparts, who have always been firmly committed to vocational education and training, even when the economy was weak. But British employers were previously cushioned by the benefits of Empire and now act within a much weaker economy, in which in particular there is a much smaller manufacturing base. This is the single most important factor in the differing cultural equation between the three countries, and it thus places their structures of education and training in a very different context.

Notwithstanding their economic advantage, there are also clearly problems with both the German and Japanese systems of education and training. The best-known is that of stress amongst Japanese school students, which is also a problem in Germany. There are frequent articles in the Press about complaining parents whose children have been told to repeat a year, or who have not been allocated by their primary teachers to the secondary school of their choice. Falling rolls aggravate this latter problem and proportions of pupils at the various types of school have undergone drastic change in favour of the grammar/Gymnasien and technical/Realschulen. This has been at the expense of the secondary modern/Hauptschulen, now down to only 40 per cent of the school population (30 per cent in West Berlin). As a result, the system has become more open to change between one type of school and another, but it is also the case that those who are placed in the lower streams within or between schools are most likely to be working-class or ethnic minority children. The odds stacked against them catching up become progressively longer.

Many German parents and teachers favour comprehensive reorganisation, while the education authorities remain firmly wedded to a tripartite system. This is legitimised by the concept of progression and supplemented by a few, largely experimental, comprehensives, most of them in Socialist-controlled regional authorities. The school system as a whole is highly competitive and produces anxiety amongst pupils and conflict between their parents and teachers. Within classrooms many teachers tend to use the marking system as their main disciplinary weapon, making behaviour as well as attainment an important factor. The result is, as one sympathetic observer noted, that 'Pupils are under great pressure to achieve demonstrably and continuously. It is not only schools, teachers, parents and job/further education prospects which create externally induced pressure. Equally significant is the process of internal socialisation in the primary school years, whereby children gradually learn to see grading as personal affirmation.'

The fact that most school-leavers have a certificate of some sort does not mean that these are of equal marketable value in the search for jobs and training. The longer apprenticeships tend to have greater worth, and youth unemployment produced the same qualification inflation in the FRG as in the UK. Not everyone gets the apprenticeship of their choice: in some regions many do not find a training place immediately, though in others more places are now offered than demanded.

School-leavers with only a Hauptschule matriculation or from special schools for those with learning difficulties, including those with German as a second language, are in the weakest position, like those in Britain with low-grade or no GCSEs. They may be helped by the Federal Education Ministry's programme for the disadvantaged, which includes help for disabled youngsters in instruction centres instead of in firms.

A foundation training year, rather like the first year of YT, has been introduced in Germany for those who do not get into the trade of their choice. This prepares young people in vocational schools for one of twelve 'vocational fields', similar in concept to the MSC's eleven Occupational Training Famil- ies. Students also brush up on their German and maths and catch up on the main school certificate if they missed it. This is all regarded as pre-vocational education and not as part of the dual vocational system.

In training, despite the large numbers of trades involved, there is a marked concentration on a few sought-after occu- pations with a distinct division between stereotypically 'male' and 'female' *Berufe*. Apprenticeships as motor mechanic, elec- trician, carpenter, painter, bricklayer, fitter or salesman are followed by nearly 40 per cent of men, while for women the concentration on a few specific trades is even greater. Nearly 60 per cent of female trainees take courses for medical assist- ants, hairdressing, bank, sales or office work. These typically 'female' occupations have, overall, an inferior qualification level to that of the typically 'male' ones. Even though girls on average obtain higher school-leaving certificates, two- thirds of those unsuccessful at gaining an apprenticeship are female.

What is also not usually mentioned is that 10 per cent of West Germans are guestworkers from Southern Europe and Turkey who do not get apprenticeships or university places. The system is thus heavily race- as well as sex-biased.

Nor is the dual system accepted without dispute in the FRG. Social Democrats and the trade unions dislike what they say is employer domination of the chambers (*Kammern*) responsible for supervising and administering training under the law. Employers suspect the Socialists of wanting to 'schoolify' the process, which reflects the fact that co-ordi- nation between school and firm is one of the major problems of the dual system. It is however made easier by the professional status accorded to instructors in the workplace, who often form joint working groups with teachers to line up the two sides of training and education.

Despite this, the dual system has not always kept sufficiently abreast of technical change to raise skill levels. Instead, de-skilling has rendered some apprenticeships time-serving activities, with the result that, as in the UK, unemployment persists alongside skill shortages.

The Greens, who represent a sizeable current of opinion in West Germany, oppose the systematised training found in the large firms but support the concept of better training in smaller companies. The other (conservative and liberal) parties tend towards the view that employers should be given more latitude to make their own training arrangements and thus reduce the educational component of the dual system. In fact, the pressure is on to reduce the length of apprenticeships. They concede however that there are those companies which do not provide adequate training. Quality of apprenticeships between large and small companies is certainly variable, with an increased share of school-based training recommended for many small firms. In sum, there is the familiar conflict between whether training should be organised according to vocational education or labour market criteria.

Scotland

In Scotland the education system has evolved separately from that in England and Wales, along with other facets of national life. The vocational system which has been created there in recent years contains much that educators and trainers south of the border can learn from. Unlike West Germany, however, Scotland's economy is weaker than England's, and the effects upon employment outcomes of a changed vocational education system can be seen in a different economic context there. The system will be described briefly because many other features are common to the rest of Britain.

School-leaving in Scotland has remained more staggered than in England and Wales because the regulations mean that around one-third of a school year group are not eligible to leave school until Christmas of the first post-compulsory year. This encourages many 16-year-olds to remain at school and merges academic and vocational subjects in post-compulsory schooling. Others leave school at Easter (approximately 14 per cent) or in the summer (43 per cent).

Another factor which has always been different from the rest of Britain is that post-compulsory schooling is organised on a yearly basis, rather than on the two years of the English sixth form. As a result, Scottish Highers, which are taken as the qualification for higher education, are broader and less specialised than the two-year A levels and higher education courses last a year longer (four years instead of three). In this respect Scottish education is closer to other European countries and to the reform of A levels regarded as desirable by many in England and Wales.

The other major difference is the complete revision of non-advanced further education that has taken place in Scotland in recent years. In 1983, Scottish education institutions faced what looked to them like a threatened take-over by the English central government in the shape of the Department of Employment's Manpower Services Commission. Unprecedented collaboration produced the Scottish Education Department's 'Action Plan' for 16–18-year-olds. This reasserted Edinburgh's leadership over its own education affairs. The Action Plan was welcomed by right and left. For the former, it integrated education and training with the demands of employers, and for the latter it represented a step towards a comprehensive education and training system up to age 18. Instead of reforming institutions, it offered a chance to change the curricula and assessment within the existing arrangements.

Following the Action Plan, all NAFE courses have been reorganised into modules of 40 hours covered by a single National Certificate of the Scottish Vocational Education Council (SCOTVEC). Assessment of the 2,000 modules so far developed is continuous and criterion-referenced. There are no grades of pass: like the National Vocational Qualifications, you either can do what is required to complete a module or you cannot. Unlike NVQs, the modules are not ordered in levels, although there are accepted routes of progression within subject areas. There is currently an effort by SCOT-VEC to line up its modules with the employer-led standards of NVQs, and SCOTVEC has a voice on the lead bodies that are developing them. But sensitivity remains about the Department of Employment-associated NCVQ taking over the Scottish system. However, with control over the vocational training programmes that used to be run by the Department's Manpower Services Commission passing to local Training and Enterprise Councils, a single system of UK (and EEC) standards and qualifications is vital to sustain coherence and comparability.

SCOTVEC National Certificate modules may be taken by full or part-time pupils, students, trainees and apprentices. They are internally assessed at schools, colleges, training centres, in work or on day-release. Consequently, relations between education and training are much more flexible and students/trainees can switch subject areas in order to collect modules to suit the requirements of their employment or their own interest. Integration of education and training is increased by the possibility of combining vocational modules with academic subjects at school or college.

However, Higher examinations still remain outside the modular system. Like the NCVQ's intention to bring professional and degree qualifications within its framework, the Action Plan proposed modularising Highers, but there is no prospect of this so long as the universities continue to withhold recognition of the National Certificate. Partly as a result, some employers tend to devalue NCs, preferring higher-status (or just more familiar) qualifications as a basis on which to make their selection for employment.

Whether because of these reforms or because of higher unemployment in the country, a larger proportion of young Scots remain in full-time education and more also join YTS than in England and Wales. As elsewhere, more young women than men pursue non-advanced further education; they therefore tend to enter employment later and fewer women are unemployed than men.

School qualifications remain critical for further advance in education or employment. The 1989 Scottish Young People's Survey concluded that better-qualified young people tend to enter the labour market at a later stage and at a higher level, or to progress to higher education. In contrast, those with lower qualifications are more likely to enter the labour market at an early stage and to join YTS (as it was then). In addition, 'Young people who became unemployed at an early stage in their careers were at a high risk of unemployment later on'. Thus the Scottish system has yet to overcome the foreclosure of possibilities for further advance created by the same 16-year parting of the ways as in England and Wales.

The outcomes of vocational education and training in the two economies of Germany and Scotland can be taken as disproving what has been called 'the training fallacy': the idea that more training will necessarily lead to more jobs. But VET should not therefore be dismissed as irrelevant. In Germany, a strong manufacturing base requires higher skill levels from its workers. Both specific vocational training and a high level of general (pre-vocational) education are needed, and employers invest in training and society in education to form a virtuous circle.

In Scotland, a greater degree of flexibility has been introduced into what was previously a very rigid, traditional system. Although this has not saved many young people from the same cut-offs that are more marked south of the Border, it is arguable that things would be even worse if the reform had not taken place. Furthermore, the Scottish system may have laid a base for further advance as the economic climate becomes more favourable.

Chapter 3

CONCLUSION: SKILLS FOR THE FUTURE

For many people interested and involved in education at whatever level, several of the developments reviewed in this book will be completely anathema and have nothing to do with what they believe education should be about. For them education is, by definition, non-vocational and concerned only with broadening the mind and developing intelligence and character.

Of course ideas are crucial to education, vocational or otherwise: new ideas are developed from experience in order to comprehend and deal with changing reality. At the present moment there is a ferment of new scientific knowledge as communications are speeded up and barriers between the disciplines disappear, and these developing ideas cannot now be relegated to antiquated subject divisions. At every level of education, new technology can be applied to facilitate learning and allow imagination a free rein beyond the immediate necessity to earn a wage and the constraints of production for profit, thus affording a vital seedbed for new ideas. Indeed, as Mrs Thatcher told the Parliamentary and Scientific Committee's fiftieth anniversary celebration: 'The greatest economic benefits of scientific research have always resulted from advances in fundamental knowledge rather than the search for specific applications.'

This space for development need not however be a vacuum, but should be related to employment and career opportunities so that people are able to see the advantages of taking up what should be their entitlement to education. The German example of meaningful qualifications related to and required for work gives some idea of how this could be achieved in practice. The aim should be to make education a lifelong process, available as of right on a lifetime basis.

The officials of the Department of Education and Science who have resurrected the traditional, subject-bound paradigm of grammar school excellence enshrined in the National Curriculum have always regarded vocational education and training as second-best. If they had acquiesced in what the Department of Employment and its Manpower Services Commission were able to do during the period of its ascendancy, it was, in the words of an often-quoted official, because they believed that 'People must once again be educated to know their place'.

But vocational education does not have to be so narrowly prescriptive. Indeed, it is hoped that enough has been said to show that all education is in fact pre-vocational, to one level or another, and that the demands which the development of technology now places upon all entrants to the workforce open up exciting possibilities for creating a new and unified system of vocational education and training. These possibilities have already been demonstrated in some of the VET programmes that have been reviewed and illustrated, and even if the best examples seem somewhat Utopian, they do at least demonstrate what can be done and point the way towards applying the same principles outside their favoured environments.

To cite an example, Letchworth in Hertfordshire may not be Utopia, but it is certainly an unusual and somewhat privileged community. It was built as the first garden city by Quakers in 1903 and its population has since expanded to 31,000. Within commuting distance of London, it is also inside the 'golden crescent' of hi-tech industrial development that stretches around the capital from Southampton to Cambridge. Unemployment is low and many people work in electronics, computing and offices, either locally or in London.

There are six secondary schools in the town, each of which has its own distinctive ethos with particular curricular strengths and specialisms. One of the two private boarding-schools is a Catholic convent, the other a vegetarian school founded to promote universal peace. All these schools are collaborating with the town corporation on a unique education experiment known as 'Education 2000', the aim of which is to attain functional literacy for the new Industrial Revolution – 'The ability to feel comfortable amidst all the changes of a highly technological democratic society – to think, communicate, collaborate and make decisions'. These are the new pre-vocational skills with which education must equip all future citizens.

For E2K, as it is known locally, computers are merely a tool to achieve this goal. The schools have them in all departments at a ratio of one computer to every ten students, and the aim is to provide one lap-top for every student within five years. These can be carried from class to class and taken home to be plugged into the project's mainframe computer. The £2 million needed for this equipment comes from industry and is not concentrated in just one centre, like a City Technology College, but spread among the schools involved.

'Time is the most vital resource you can buy. It is more important than technology', says an information technology co-ordinator at one of Letchworth's four comprehensive schools.

'I was self-taught basically. I was loaned a machine to take home and given time to attend a course at the local further education college. Now I spend half my time training other teachers in the school. Each department gets a double period timetabled training per week with double that for the special needs department.'

'Computing has changed everybody's teaching. You can't give traditional lessons any more. It's made us much more organised. The library, for instance, wasn't really used before. Now it's the centre of information technology in the school and the community. It's not only hardware and software. The underlying thing is changing people's attitudes to learning.'

As well as an IT co-ordinator, each school has a community co-ordinator. 'Our job', explained one, 'is to teach people to recognise educational experiences. There are lots of people outside school who can, often unwittingly, become teachers.

Some parents are now beginning to walk in and out of school as if they own the place, which of course they do. At the same time, a much greater trust has developed between students and teachers. It's become a mutual learning process.'

E2K began in Letchworth with meetings where students were encouraged to define their own educational needs in line with the project's aim of allowing people to take responsibility for their own learning. One of the striking findings to emerge at this preliminary stage was that young people, while they want recognition of their own particular needs, do not always necessarily want separate facilities from adults but often prefer integration with them. John Abbott, the Director of E2K, has a vision of learning centres in the town, of which schools would be but one; others would be attached to doctors' surgeries or in factories and community centres. Amongst them, schools could become role models of continuous change for an educative community.

The project has begun to establish study groups which involve teachers with local community organisations. Through a programme of industrial placements, teachers have also become familiar with the opportunities for their pupils and parents in local industry and commerce. A network of local companies also support work experience for students, where they can see the use to which the information technology they work with in school is put. The students will already be familiar with databases, spreadsheets, computer-aided design and the other computer facilities which increasingly give them the ability and confidence to manage their own learning, to solve practical problems and to communicate their ideas – the very qualities which industry claims it requires.

In Hampshire, one of the largest local education authorities in England intends to give every pupil in its 114 secondary schools and sixth-form colleges access to modern computer systems. To do this it is spending £10 million over five years, with a further £5 million for its junior schools, a requirement of £3 million additional spending per year to reach the ratio of eight pupils per computer. (At least, this was the intention until local management of schools, and a 40 per cent cut in the educational support grant which the government gives LEAs for IT, threw the strategy into confusion.)

Close links with industry are regarded as a key factor in Hampshire's information technology strategy for schools. The Post Office, which has its IT Division in Farnborough, invested £65,000 in a local comprehensive school for a purpose-built IT suite. The Chairman of the Post Office, Sir Bryan Nicholson, former head of the old Manpower Services Commission, made it clear that 'The aim is more general than producing dozens of apprentice IT specialists . . . Its real value will only come if it encourages other businesses to form similar partnerships with other schools.'

Professor Tom Stonier of Bradford University's Department of Science and Society has calculated the costs of providng all children in Britain with a computer system to be used at home and at school. '£200 per personal system should buy a lot', he reckons.

> It should include a small portable keyboard which could be carried back and forth the way one carries books. A modem at home to plug into the telephone system and similar devices at school. Disc drives, printing facilities for home and school, and other peripherals in schools ranging from remote-controlled turtles and other robots, to sophisticated software, hard-disc back-up and expert system facilities. If spread over a six-year period, this would run to approximately £500 million a year or 5 per cent of the present education budget.
>
> As a result, the country would become truly computerate, for you would be getting such equipment into the vast majority of homes. The amount of commercial activity generated in terms of hardware and software production, servicing, training, etc., would provide a further instructive stimulus to the economy and create the kind of intellectual infrastructure to assure a technologically literate society in the next century.

The release of facilities in schools and colleges caused by the drop in numbers of teenagers creates opportunities for providing education and training for the 70 per cent of the current workforce who have not acquired any vocational qualifications, as well as the two million and more people still unemployed. With investment in the technology, schools and colleges could respond to the gathering pace of technological change which requires a corresponding programme of retraining throughout employees' careers. Technological change is accelerating exponentially to link, transfer, store and retrieve knowledge through computers and telecommunications, and since education essentially deals with communicating knowledge, it cannot remain uninvolved. Education is the single most important investment in the knowledge industry that is suppposed to be shifting the economy of the developed world from an industrial to an information base.

Yet a redirection of resources to enable schools to give all their pupils the pre-vocational skills necessary for full computer literacy would still only provide the technical potential to create a new and unified system of vocational education and training. A new curriculum which facilitates transfer between its different levels is also required. 'The challenge of ever implementing that proposal would be formidable', commented Professor Tony Edwards, who proposed such a 'Reconstruction of Education and Training' in 1983, 'less for its cost than its contradiction of deeply grooved hierarchies of "the educated", "the trained" and "the workers".'

For the opportunities that it would provide to be real, the social divisions that have too often been reinforced by the old separated education and training systems will have to be overcome. It has been argued that the 'differentiation' which it is the declared object of the latest education reforms to accentuate can only widen these divisions.

Even during the vocational phase of education policy from 1976 to 1987, too many programmes for relating education to work and for developing training were conceived as being for other people's children. Too often, training programmes were designed less to equip their participants for work than temporarily to disguise their more or less permanent unemployment. Now, even what were often − despite the best efforts of many of those involved − only pretences at training,

121

have been abandoned. Training has been replaced by enterprise.

'Enterprise', declares the Training Agency, 'will play an important role in restructuring the British economy, starting small businesses, reviving the inner cities and expanding European markets in 1992.' It has been seen how Enterprise in Higher Education was defined to mean the pre-vocational skills now required of higher-level managerial and administrative personnel working in a demand-flexible environment; also how higher education was itself expected to become enterprising enough to sell its services to its consumers, dismantling its traditional structures in the process.

The enterprising skills of self-presentation in order to sell your services on an individual contractual basis are rapidly extending to all employees. A recent study of microprocessor manufacture noted, 'What seems to be emerging in some of the "pioneering" plants is an attempt to uncouple an individual's pay from the going rate for the job . . . negotiating with each worker individually. This strategy means that rewards are not simply determined by job content or technical skill but, also, by the behavioural skill of an individual.'

Enterprise skills have been identified by one of their enthusiastic advocates as comprising variously: 'Initiative, persuasive powers, risk-taking ability, flexibility, creativity, independence, problem-solving, need for achievement, imagination, belief in control over one's own destiny, leadership, hard work' (*Enterprise Culture – Its Meaning and Implications for Education and Training* by Allan Gibb).

Clearly, as the author's fellow professor at Durham University, Frank Coffield, says, 'We are not dealing here with a tightly defined unitary concept but with a farrago of "hurrah" words'. Beyond these skills of self-presentation there are the skills of transforming materials, relating to one another and to the world around us, and developing new ideas from experience so as to avoid repeating past errors. Society depends upon these real skills, and they should not be forgotten as training gives way to enterprise.

Local Training and Enterprise Councils have now taken

over the £3 billion annual training budget. This spells the end of the attempt to create a coherent national training system. The TECs are dominated by the same private-sector employers who, as the MSC stated in 1981, 'perceive training as a disposable overhead dropped at the first sight of lowering profit margins'. Yet they have also been given an increased say in running the polytechnics and universities, FE colleges and schools.

With these entrepreneurs' renewed enthusiasm for enterprise, there is a danger that any notion of real skills in training and education will be rapidly lost, even though those same employers have never ceased to complain of skill shortages which are now, after all the money that has been spent over the years on skill training, reaching crisis proportions. It is therefore important to keep hold of an idea of what skill really is.

Skill can be defined as the ability to manage uncertainty. Apart from the skills of traditional handicrafts, those most highly valued by society are diagnostic skills. The mechanic who can test and analyse a car engine in order to find its faults is obviously more skilled than the fitter whose only task is to fit exhausts in a drive-in centre. Similarly, the systems analysts who devise and test new computer programs are more skilled than the operators who merely follow the system once it has been installed. The proverbial brain surgeon also combines book knowledge acquired through theoretical study with manual dexterity developed by long practice.

Artists and scientists also combine manual and mental skills in the processes of creation and discovery. They often use sophisticated equipment, while employing a high degree of theoretical abstraction and creative intuition. The vital role played by such 'pure' research and its creative application in the development of the computer industry is well documented. Transistors from wave mechanics and solid state physics, nuclear energy from Einstein's formulations are other examples.

123

The effects of the introduction of new technology in engineering, according to a survey undertaken for the MSC, is that

> In many fields knowledge over a broad range of disciplines is sought with more emphasis being placed on diagnostic competence. For example, technologists increasingly find themselves fulfilling part-managerial functions and work in multi-disciplinary environments. A broader range of competence and systems awareness is also demanded of technicians and the demand for multi-skilled craft workers is sustained.
>
> The existing classifications of occupations as craftsmen, technicians, technologists and engineers already seem inappropriate in the light of the changes wrought by new technology. The enlargement of some jobs in clerical and administrative occupations to include other skills, such as social skills needed for selling and counselling, means that existing classifications fail to categorise new jobs properly.

There are four processes occurring simultaneously to skill levels as new technology is applied to work or, as microelectronic control systems and telematic communications are doing, diffuses itself throughout society:

Enskilling extends and develops existing skills in a minority of specialised areas.

Multi-skilling retains existing skills while combining them with new skills in other areas. (In flexible manufacturing an overall knowledge of and ability to operate anywhere in the complete process is known as 'systems competence'.)

Re-skilling involves learning new skills to the same level of uncertainty as the ones they replace.

De-skilling means that the skills that would formerly have been acquired are lost; instead, lower-level skills in a number of formerly discrete areas are acquired to gain the 'core skills' necessary for semi-skilled working.

It is not inevitable that the majority of the workforce need to be de-skilled and relegated to a periphery of semi-skilled, intermittent labour by a securely employed minority who manipulate information by using the latest electronic communications and control systems. Rather than dividing and directing intensified labour into isolated and repetitive jobs, new technology has the potential to lighten and diversify work, which is in fact its most effective use.

Larry Hirschhorn describes a factory in America using computer-integrated manufacture where 'The computer answers queries put to it by operating personnel regarding the short-run effects of variables at various control levels, but decisions are made by the operators. Operating personnel are provided with technical calculations and economic data conventionally only available to technical staff, that support learning and self-regulation. In this manner operator learning is enhanced.'

The development of new technology has the potential not only to simplify tasks but also for them to be shared and integrated, thereby increasing productivity with less laborious and repetitive effort. It thus presents a real opportunity for the transformation of the ancient division of labour between workers by hand and by brain. To take full advantage of this historic opportunity requires a new arrangement of education and training. Unlike the latest reforms being attempted in the schools system, this would not try to return to the type of selective organisation that existed in the past. Rather, for the first time, formal, academic study needs to be intimately related with practical, applied learning in a unified system of vocational education and training.

This new education/training system would demolish the traditional divisions between an elite education for the professions and practical training for the crafts. Such a unified system of modernised schooling and apprenticeship would undermine and eventually break down the class barriers that are sustained by an outdated division of labour at work. At the same time, new and more equal social relations could only promote the modernisation and revitalisation of the economy.

If new technology is to be used to its fullest advantage and achieve its potential of effecting a new industrial revolution, vocational education and training has to be extended as universally as possible. This could be achieved through a new, integrated education and training curriculum and within a unified credit transfer system for all post-16 courses, which would overcome traditional divisions between unskilled, semi-skilled and skilled workers and the new core/periphery division. Together with co-ordinated in-house training at the workplace, it would contribute towards creating a flexible and multi-skilled craft workforce. All members of this workforce would combine the mental skills of diagnosis and programming with the manual abilities to effect repairs and maintain production.

This implies that it will also be necessary to obliterate the distinction between blue- and white-collar workers, between the office and the plant, between managers and managed, between those who think and those who do. In turn this requires a complete transformation of existing attitudes towards education and training, which can no longer be regarded as separate and insular compartments. Instead, they must be seen as indistinguishable and permanent processes which have to be continued throughout everyone's working lives.

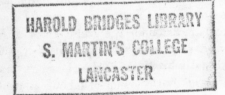

BIBLIOGRAPHY

For a general guide to the present situation in education: Bash, L. and Coulby, D. *The Education Reform Act: Competition and Control* (Cassell, 1989).

See the other titles in the Education Matters series for closer examination of different aspects of the new order as they affect schools.

For a guide to the Act itself: Simon, B. *Bending the Rules: the Baker 'Reform' of Education* (Lawrence and Wishart, 1988);

and for a very readable account of the political events leading up to its passage: Jones, K. *Right Turn: the Conservative Revolution in Education* (Hutchinson Radius, 1989); also

Morris, M. and Griggs, C. *Education: the Wasted Years? 1973–1986* (Falmer, Brighton, 1988), particularly George Low's witty essay on the Manpower Services Commission.

On the part played by the Manpower Services Commission in particular: Ainley, P. and Corney, M. *Training for the Future: the Rise and Fall of the Manpower Services Commission* (Cassell, 1990); while Benn, C. and Fairley, J. (eds) *Challenging the MSC on Jobs, Training and Education* (Pluto, 1986) provides a critical response to the MSC's dominance of VET during the period. So does the

National Labour Movement Inquiry into Youth Unemployment and Training (Birmingham Trades Council Union Resource Centre, 1987).

On the history of training in Britain, the standard account is Perry, P. *The Evolution of British Manpower Policy* (British Association for Commercial and Industrial Education, 1974).

See also the excellent though brief Sheldrake, J. and Vickerstaff, S. *The History of Industrial Training in Britain* (Avebury, Godstone, Surrey, 1987).

The classic account of how things used to be is Carter, M. *Home, School and Work: a Study of the Education and Employment of Young People in Britain* (Pergamon, Oxford, 1962).

Present government training policy is outlined in the White Paper *Employment for the 1990s* (HMSO, 1988).

Burke, John W. (ed.) *Competency Based Education and Training*

(Falmer, Lewes, 1989) points towards likely future developments; and

Gleeson, Denis (ed.) *Training and its Alternatives* (Open University Press, Milton Keynes, 1990) offers some different possibilities.

Crucial documents stating past policies and priorities are:

Department of Education and Science, *Education and Training for Young People* (Cmnd 9482) and *Better Schools* (Cmnd 9469) (HMSO, 1985);

Department of Employment, White Paper *Training and Jobs* (HMSO, 1984);

Manpower Services Commission, *A New Training Initiative: an Agenda for Action* (Cmnd 8455; HMSO, 1981) and *Towards a Comprehensive Manpower Policy* (HMSO, 1976);

Training for Skill Ownership in the Youth Training Scheme (Institute of Manpower Studies, Brighton, 1983); and

Further Education Unit, *A Basis for Choice* (DES, 1979).

Manpower Services Commission, *Competence and Competition* (HMSO, 1985) stimulated foreign comparisons, especially with West Germany; see further:

Taylor, M. *Education and Work in the Federal Republic of Germany* (Anglo-German Foundation for the Study of Industrial Society, London, 1981);

Her Majesty's Inspectorate, *Education in the Federal Republic of Germany: Aspects of Curriculum and Assessment* (DES/HMSO, 1986);

and for a criticism see Chisholm, L. 'Vorsprung Ex Machina? Aspects of Curriculum and Assessment in Cultural Comparison', *Journal of Education Policy*, vol. 2, no. 2 (1987).

For Scotland see Raffe, D. (ed.) *Fourteen to Eighteen: the Changing Pattern of Schooling in Scotland* (Aberdeen University Press, 1989).

On Education 2000: Fisher, P. *Education 2000: Mixing Educational Change with Consent* (Cassell, 1990).

The Department of Employment's *Employment Gazette* publishes regular updates of the employment and training situation; see also Youthaid's *Working Brief* and the Unemployment Unit's *Bulletin*, published regularly from 9 Poland Street, London W1V 3DG.

David Lodge's novel (and subsequent television series) *Nice Work* wittily describes some of the unintended consequences of industrial and academic integration; and Dickens' *Nicholas Nickleby* and *Hard Times* respectively contain the archetypes of vocational and academic education in Dotheboys Hall and the M'Choakumchild School, Coketown.

More generally on art, craft, skill and work:

Coleman, R. *The Art of Work: an Epitaph to Skill* (Pluto, 1988);

Cooley, M. *Architect or Bee? The Human Price of Technology* (Hogarth Press, 1987);

Handy, C. *The Future of Work* (Martin Robertson, Oxford, 1984);

Hirschhorn, L. *Beyond Mechanisation: Work and Technology in a Post-Industrial Age* (MIT, Boston, Massachusetts, 1984);

Pye, D. *The Nature and Art of Workmanship* (Cambridge University Press, 1968).

INDEX

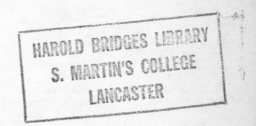